Marketing Express

JOHN L. MARIOTTI

Published in 2006 by Capstone Publishing Ltd. (A Wiley company), The Atrium,
Southern Gate Chichester, West Sussex, PO19 8SQ, England

Phone (+44) 1243 779777

Email (for orders and customer service enquiries): cs-books@wiley.co.uk
Visit our Home Page on www.wiley.co.uk or www.wiley.com

Reprinted April 2006

Other Wiley Editorial Offices

John Wiley & Sons Inc., 111 River Street, Hoboken, NJ 07030, USA

Jossey-Bass, 989 Market Street, San Francisco, CA 94103-1741, USA

Wiley-VCH Verlag GmbH, Boschstr. 12, D-69469 Weinheim, Germany

John Wiley & Sons Australia Ltd, 42 McDougall Street, Milton, Queensland 4064, Australia

John Wiley & Sons (Asia) Pte Ltd, 2 Clementi Loop #02-01, Jin Xing Distripark, Singapore 129809

John Wiley & Sons Canada Ltd, 22 Worcester Road, Etobicoke, Ontario, Canada M9W 1L1

Wiley also publishes its books in a variety of electronic formats. Some content that appears
in print may not be available in electronic books.

CIP Catalogue records for this book are available from the British Library and the US Library of Congress

ISBN 10: 1-84112-704-3 (PB) ISBN 13: 978-1-84112-704-0 (PB)

Typeset in 9/11pt Garamond by Laserwords Private Limited, Chennai, India
Printed and bound in Great Britain by TJ International, Padstow, Cornwall
This book is printed on acid-free paper responsibly manufactured from sustainable forestry
in which at least two trees are planted for each one used for paper production.

Contents

01

Introduction

This explains why marketing and marketing strategy is so important to managers in the 21st century.

Why do companies exist? What is business all about? Noted authority Theodore Levitt says, *"the purpose of a business is to create and keep a customer."* I think he's on the right track. Companies and businesses exist because someone had a need (or a "want") and someone else fulfilled that need with a product or service. How did that person know such a need existed? How did s/he develop a product or service that met that need? And how did they communicate that such a product or service existed? Then, how was the original person with a need convinced to buy this particular product, when there were many others that were similar and might have fulfilled the need?

The answers are Marketing, Marketing, Marketing, and . . . Marketing. Do you think marketing is important? It is only the beginning of everything. An old saying states that *"nothing happens until a sale is made,"* and that is true. But until someone does some marketing, there is nothing to sell, and no premise on which to sell it. There is even very little knowledge about who to sell it to.

Marketing is the eyes and ears of the company, tuned to the customer, and to competition. Marketing is the driving force behind new products, behind the promotion and advertising and all of the other communications about those new products. Marketing's job, in the words of another well-known expert, Roger Blackwell, is simply *"to have what will sell."* What a wonderfully elegant and simple way to say it. But as in all wonderfully simple seeming things, there is a veritable forest of complexity just below the surface, and that is what this book will explore.

"Having what will sell" means so many things. It means having the product or service that a specific market segment wants, at a price they will find attractive compared to alternative choices. "Having what will sell" also means having distribution channels that will have the product in stock and available for purchase through the channels of distribution that those customers normally use. It also means communicating to prospective purchasers that the product or service exists, why it is the most desirable alternative to buy, and how to obtain it - and this is no small task.

Finally, "having what will sell" means fulfilling or exceeding the purchaser's expectations. You must first fulfill the order itself, either directly or through a system of distribution. You must next fulfill the promise that the communications, advertising, promotion or brand name (and image) conveyed to the purchaser. In most cases, it was this promise that actually created the sale. Then, having sold the product, you must be ready to provide any necessary after sales service. This might be an accessory to use with the product; it might mean instructions or clarification on how to use the service or product properly; it might mean standing behind the product in the event of a problem - usually called a warranty.

Last, but certainly not least, there must be a relationship of some sort between the creator, seller and buyer of a product or service. Above all else, marketing is all about creating, supporting and building that relationship so it can become the basis for repeat sales and a continuing business. To succeed in the future, by doing superb marketing, you simply must "have what will sell!" Isn't it simple?

In the course of expanding on these ideas, there will be many examples used to illustrate how companies successfully use marketing to great advantage. If the examples are familiar, that is because successful marketing tends to make its user somewhat "famous." Familiar examples are also helpful because they are just that - "familiar" - and most readers will easily relate to the product or service involved.

Are you ready? Here we go on the Marketing Express! All aboard!

02

Definition of Terms

This chapter covers key concepts that help in defining the field of marketing and its strategy. A number of marketing issues are discussed with the actions that are necessary to deal with them.

MARKETING – ONE DEFINITION

Marketing is the practice of understanding the needs and wants of customers, discovering or creating products/services that meet those customers' needs and wants, and then communicating this internally to the organization which must create and deliver the products/services and externally to the customers for whom they are intended, so they will desire them and buy them.

> "Marketing is the process by which decisions are made in a totally interrelated changing business environment on all the activities that facilitate exchange in order that a targeted group of customers are satisfied and the defined objectives accomplished."
>
> *Robert D. Hisrich, Marketing*

WHAT MARKETING IS *NOT*

Marketing is not sales. Sales is different in that it involves the presentation of the outcomes of marketing's efforts. This does not mean that marketing never sells anything – it does. But it primarily sells concepts and plans, more than specific products. Marketing is not R&D or Product Development either. These are the idea-grounds and the implementers of what will meet the customer needs and wants which were discovered and communicated by marketing. Finally, marketing is not Logistics. Logistics is the deployment of people and resources to assure that the materials needed are in the right place and the right time, with the necessary information to assure fulfillment of the customer's orders.

Marketing is a truly a series of different but inter-related functions, each of which must be carefully and closely integrated with the others if the final outcome – *"having what you can sell"* – is to be achieved.

STRATEGY IS WHERE MARKETING STARTS

The first important point about marketing is that strategy and marketing are inextricably intertwined. A business must start with a strategy. That strategy is usually built on answers to a few simple questions. (Only the questions are simple - the answers usually aren't!) When the time comes to translate that strategy to marketing, here's the key question: "What do we want to sell, to whom, where, and how?"

Once that has been asked, and answered, the real work of marketing can begin. When I talk about "products" I also mean services or combinations of a product and a service. I will revisit this topic of strategy repeatedly because, in the real world, the question will need to be asked repeatedly as you adapt time and again to changes in competition, situations, information and constraints. Often there is a core idea, perhaps a proprietary technology, or a crying need for something - a product or a service. Once this idea exists, marketing can run with it. The Palm Pilot, the Polaroid instant camera, and digital cellular phones are examples of solutions to consumer needs and wants based on specific technologies.

Answer the "what" questions

Deciding what will sell is not obvious. There are many occasions when it should be simple for marketing to know what will sell. There are records of what has sold in the past and market research information about what customers and consumers think - or at least what they said they thought. (Careful, these two things are not always the same!) The problem is that everything marketing people know is about the past or based on conjecture on the part of others, and everything that will happen occurs in the future, which is uncertain. These make the "what" decision much tougher than it appears on the surface.

> "The new game of strategy is not playing within a boundary, but playing with the boundary - how to change the boundary . . . When anyone plays with the boundaries, there is no longer a clearly defined or predetermined turf."
>
> *C.K. Prahalad, co-author, Competing for the Future. Harvard Business School Press*

There are a couple of other things that a marketer needs to know about answering the "what to sell" question. The first is that market boundaries are more blurred than ever. No longer can you find nice neat pieces of markets to target. Think about telephones. It used to be a pretty straightforward market. There was an instrument that sat on your desk plugged into the wall and had either a dial or pushbuttons on it. Pick it up, hear a dial tone, and start dialing or pushing buttons.

Now the question of where the boundaries of the phone market are - if there are any - is very complex. Cordless phones, cell phones, two-way pagers, satellite phones, PDAs with built in satellite links, computers with infrared and RF ports, two-way radios, and Internet telephony are only some of the parts of what was the telephone market - in addition to the old wired phones, which still exist. So, if you want to sell the phone market, the next questions are which segment of it, how broadly, etc. Define your market carefully and stay flexible as conditions change. It may need to be redefined.

> "Value is shifting from companies that provide products to companies that can provide high customization at low cost (Dell) or who are solutions providers (IBM)."
>
> *Dr Philip Kotler, Northwestern University*

Answering the "what to sell" question is an iterative process. Answer it, then test the market and adjust. Then do it again and again. Answering this question is important because it determines where you will focus resources. Focus is an important concept. Both human and financial resources are limited, so directing those valuable resources at anything but the center of the market target might mean wasting them, or at least not getting the best results. Bottom line: make sure you think carefully about *what* to sell, and be ready to adjust, as more information becomes available. Also, make sure your *company's strategy* is clear on this issue!

> "One of the major issues marketers face is the increasing reliance of consumers and prospects on perceptions rather than facts when making purchasing decisions."
>
> *Don E. Schultz, Stanley I. Tannenbaum and Robert F. Lauterborn, The New Marketing Paradigm, NTC Business Books, Chicago, IL, 1993*

Next decide "to whom and where"

If you can answer the "what" questions, then come the "to whom, where," and a little later, the "how" questions. Marketing's job is understanding what goes on in the mind of customers and consumers and then translating that into products and services priced to sell and delivered to satisfy - no, better yet - to excite and delight the consumer. After all, you want them to come back and buy from you again! Deciding "to whom" to sell a product is perhaps marketing's most critical job (assuming that your company has already decided the "what"). Pick the *target market* well (that's what we call the "whom"), and you have a chance to succeed. Pick it poorly and you will almost certainly fail.

As a start, let's make sure we have the terminology straight. Customers are the people who buy the product or service from you. They pay your company for whatever they buy. Consumers may or may not be your direct customers. If you sell to a retailer or distributor, the end consumer is the end user. It might be a consumer who buys at the retail store, or it might be the company who buys from the distributor. The same goes for services.

The "where" is sort of a dependent question. "Where" can mean the geographic location of the chosen target market customers. It can also mean the scope of the geography you choose to target. Deciding "where" is important because it is also about focus. In fact, much of marketing is a matter of focus. Focus means deciding where you are going to spend resources to get results, and then measuring how you did, adjusting and trying again until you get it right - or run out of resources - at which point you might need to update your résumé.

THE ESSENCE OF MARKETING[1]

- The purpose of a business is to create and keep a customer.
- To do that you have to produce and deliver goods and services that people want and value at prices and under conditions that are reasonably attractive relative to those offered by others to a proportion of customers large enough to make those prices and conditions possible.
- To continue to do that, the enterprise must produce revenues in excess of costs in sufficient quantity and with sufficient regularity to attract and hold investors and at least keep abreast and sometimes ahead of competitors.
- No enterprise, no matter how small, can do any of this by mere instinct or accident. It has to clarify its purpose, strategies, and plans and the larger the enterprise, the more important that these be written, clearly communicated and frequently updated by management.
- In all cases there must be an appropriate system of measures, rewards, and controls to assure that what is intended gets done and when that doesn't happen, that corrective action is taken.

THE MARKETING PLAN

The name we use for the tool that is most commonly used to describe how these different inter-related functions are to be integrated is the *marketing plan*. The marketing plan takes many forms, but the most common is a written document which outlines the key elements that must be considered and then implemented. There are lots of formats for marketing plans. Some come in textbooks and software packages, and others have evolved over a period of years at leading companies.

I won't get hung up on the format. That's the easier part, and many companies already have one they want to use. The harder part is what goes in the marketing plan and how/why those pieces work together to come up with *"what you can sell, to whom, where and how."* One point is very important – the marketing plan does need to be *written*, and it must be done clearly and concisely. If it isn't, it cannot be easily communicated, and it will be of no use to many of the key people who must understand it, but were not involved in its development.

A good marketing plan begins with *strategy*, and strategy begins with a careful *assessment of the current situation* in your chosen market or market segment. That's a big sentence. "Careful assessment" means *really thinking* about what's going on in the current situation. Too many people deceive themselves about how strong or weak their company is or how good or bad the competitors are. The result is a plan that is destined to fail because it is built on erroneous assumptions.

A *clear understanding* of the current *reality* is critical at the outset. Sometimes that means getting outside help to form objective conclusions. Companies usually over-react or under-react to competition. If competition is doing well, it is easy to over-estimate how good it is. If competition is doing poorly, it is even easier to under-estimate them.

> "The leaders in real time management will constantly monitor even the most minute changes."
> *Regis McKenna, Real Time, Harvard Business School Press, Boston, 1997*

WHO, WHAT, WHERE, HOW...?

The "chosen market or market segment" is a challenging set of words because it requires that conscious choices be made. As I stated earlier, *defining the target market/segment* is often the hardest and most critical thing to do in a marketing plan. It is also the critical starting place.

Often, after a careful assessment (thought) has been made of the current situation, the choice of which markets to serve may become more evident. While it sounds obvious, it is desirable to serve markets that are more readily accessible and in which strong competition is absent. Of course those are hard to find! Some real innovation may be required! Taking on well-entrenched competitors in slow-growing markets is not very much fun – and it is usually far less profitable than growing in newer, less competitive markets.

Significant growth can only come from doing four things:

- target markets that are growing faster than the norm;
- find new products (or services) to sell into established markets;
- find new markets (or geography) to sell established products; and
- innovate and introduce products (or services) that expand the market.

The most fun place to go after sales growth is in a new, rapidly growing, and profitable market. Obvious statement? Sure. But look around at how many companies slog along in low profit markets growing at 1–2% or less (or even declining due to deflationary pricing), and try to generate sales growth at double-digit rates. Even to a novice marketer, this must seem silly.

To grow in mature, slow-growth markets, you simply have to take share from competitors who are trying to do the same thing to you. Or, if you are really original and take the advice of gurus like Gary Hamel and C.K. Prahalad, you need to exercise some "industry foresight." Hamel admonishes you to become revolutionaries, and rule breakers, but this is very hard or impossible while working (and peacefully coexisting) within the walls of comfortably profitable industry incumbents.

To grow faster than a mature market, long term, you have to redefine the market, expand the market, and generally start a revolution. When you do that, profit growth can (doesn't necessarily) come along – and it's your job as an aspiring revolutionary marketer to be sure that it does. Everyone from your president to the union rep, from the engineers to the janitor should like that. With more profit, there is simply more wealth to spread around.

To marketers, profit is certainly not a dirty word! It is a wonderful word, because it also guarantees that you will have a chance to compete another day. Profit comes most easily when you have proprietary products in areas that are growing rapidly and have not yet been overpopulated with competitors. For the majority of companies, these kinds of opportunities are few and far between – but that is no reason to stop looking for them.

Once the marketing plan has outlined what markets/segments to serve, etc., then it is time to move on to a couple of other important decision areas. Exactly what combinations of products and/or services will you sell to these chosen markets, at what kind of pricing, profit margins, and in what kind of product line structures? These are critical decisions because the choices made here determine how direct the competition will be and how profitable success will turn out to be.

There are very few product or service categories that consist of a single product offering. Multiple offerings in a category help avoid commoditization. Multiple offerings help provide added opportunities for differentiation and with differentiation comes opportunities for increased profitability. Many companies are also successfully bundling products and services at far better profitability than selling the products alone. The potential for market growth, penetration, and profitability lies in finding the right variations to match what the end user consumers will prefer and pay for.

This leads to the next part of the marketing plan, which is the market opportunity analysis and market research. It is absolutely amazing how often people attempt to enter markets or make plans for growth in sales without even fully understanding where the opportunities lie, who has the volume now, how entrenched the competitors are with desired customers, and so forth. It is really surprising how little some companies know when they venture into a market - and blunders are common in these circumstances. *Ignorance is NOT bliss* - at least not in marketing.

> "There is no such thing as a commodity. All goods and services can be differentiated and usually are."
>
> *Theodore Levitt, The Marketing Imagination*

But do not despair, because there are several excellent tools that can help with market opportunity analysis and identification of competitive situations. I have listed a couple of these in the Resources chapter. Well-planned and professionally executed market research can provide useful information about how to go to market and gain competitive advantage against the current incumbents - *but you have to move fast*, because someone else is probably targeting the same market as you are, especially if it is an attractive one.

Before I leave this chapter, let me summarize the typical topics that make up a marketing plan. This can be a useful checklist for developing a good marketing plan.

> "The competitive environment will no longer tolerate slow response or delayed decision making."
>
> *Regis McKenna, Real Time*

WHAT THE *COMPLETE* MARKETING PLAN MUST CONTAIN – A CHECKLIST ANSWERING A CRITICAL QUESTION:

"What do we want to sell to whom, where, how, when, and how much, and where will we get it, and can we make money at it?"

Markets

» Market definition(s) with size and growth rate(s)
» Target segment(s) and customer(s) with size and growth rate(s)
» Current and projected situation analysis
» Market opportunity analysis
» Competitive analysis
» Market research (required to verify)

Products

» Product/service definition(s)
» Features and specifications
» Product line structure

Sales

» Strategies ("what" statements)
» Implementation steps ("how" statements)
» Tactics or operational action plans
» Sales strategies

Promotional

» Communications plan
» Advertising and promotion Plans (initial and follow-on support)
» Packaging, collateral materials and POP support
» Launch plans, timing and resources

» Milestones, measures and feedback methods
» Product/service acquisition, delivery and logistics*

Operational
» Sourcing plans
» Production plans
» Distribution plans
» Order fulfillment plans
» After-sales customer service

Economic
» Feasibility and viability
» Economic analysis (to justify the investment and get the money!)
» Return on investment
» Mix and margin analyses - initial and ongoing
» Budgets - expense and capital

*Note: May be furnished from outside marketing organization.

NOTE

1 Levitt, T. (1983) and (1986) *The Marketing Imagination*. The Free Press, New York.

03

The Evolution of Marketing

This chapter explains how marketing evolved from its earliest roots, including the effects of advancements in transportation and mass communications media. It also frames the marketing issues of brand development, in the era of globalization and the Internet.

IN THE OLDEN DAYS

To understand the evolution of marketing, let's go back in time to the early 1800s or even much earlier. The markets of that era weren't nearly so specialized as those areas we consider markets today. In fact, marketing was simply a byproduct of earning a living. Most people were employed in either agricultural work (farming, raising animals, etc.) or in crafts and trades necessary to manufacture things people used in day-to-day life, or in the conduct of commerce. These craftsmen created some of the earliest brands in the form of marks they put on their work to identify whose product it was. Some of the earliest forms of marketing were no more complicated than the sign in front of their shop, which announced their name, their craft/trade or both. This was all they needed - then.

It shouldn't be surprising that many of the surnames of people we find in much of the Western world are based on the crafts or trades of their family predecessors. Think about the fact that in times gone by people might be known as "John the Baker" or "Charles the Shoemaker." This was all the identification they needed. In later times these names would be shortened to "John Baker," "Charles Shoemaker," and so forth. Marketing was pretty straightforward. If you wanted some grain milled, you probably went to "Edward the Miller," and later on to Ed Miller and maybe even later to Miller's Grain Company!

THE PRINTED WORD

Now let's continue our journey through time from the past to the future. When the printing press was invented in 1455, a whole new way of reproducing text-based information came into being. The later invention of mass-produced paper made it possible for the word to be spread far and wide by the circulation of printed material. At this point in history, the slow forms of transportation still limited the spread of printed information. While wandering peddlers might carry printed material with them, it was often very difficult to purchase goods from faraway craftsmen. Then, as always seems to happen, a few breakthroughs altered the landscape of marketing and commerce.

If you go back far enough, to the era before the invention of the printing press, most of the written word was produced in the form of books, created by monks in monasteries, laboriously hand copying the text. It was not all that common for most people even to know how to read and write. Thus traditional written forms of marketing that we consider commonplace were not even used. Handbills were one of the first forms of distance marketing, but these also had to travel by riders on horses, or overland carriages (often called stagecoaches in the US). Then there was the problem of traveling to make the purchase and bring it back with you.

SLOW COMMUNICATIONS

Communications of a century ago were very slow - usually limited to the distance a person walking or riding a horse could travel in a given amount of time. Because transportation was limited to walking or riding a horse (or using a horse and buggy), people would seldom travel further than necessary from their home to obtain the necessities of life. This made marketing in that era a decidedly local, word of mouth practice. People made plans and communicated their purchase intentions via word of mouth. If the craftsman's work was worthy and of good value then word of it spread from purchaser to purchaser. A smart marketer can learn a lot from this age-old lesson.

There is still nothing like word of mouth testimonial to spread the knowledge and desirability of a product or service. There is another side to this, however, because studies have proven that failures of products and services are passed on by word of mouth at least five to ten times as often as successes. Therein lies the opportunity and the challenge for marketers. As technology progressed, the next major events that dramatically influenced marketing were the application of the steam engine to the development of railroads and trains, and the development of the telegraph.

> "Over the course of a few years, a new communications technology annihilated distance and shrank the world faster and farther than ever before. A world-wide communications network whose cables spanned continents and oceans, it

revolutionized business practices and gave rise to new forms of crime."

The subject: not the Internet, but the telegraph, in 1840.

The first message: "What hath God wrought?"

The railroads made possible a quantum leap in the speed and distance a person or goods could travel in a given amount of time. They provided a means of conveying products to purchasers in faraway places. Around the same time that the railroads developed, the second part of that revolution came into widespread use - the telegraph.

The telegraph was the first means for information to travel further and faster than a person could travel (well, with the exception of homing pigeons, which were not particularly reliable and had a very limited payload). This meant that information could be at the person's destination before they got there. While the Morse code used in the telegraph was unwieldy for use as a marketing tool, the sheer magnitude of this leap in communications changed the world of commerce dramatically.

"E-commerce is to the Information Revolution what the railroad was to the Industrial Revolution - a new, unprecedented, and unexpected development."
Peter F. Drucker, "Knowledge Work." Executive Excellence, April 2000

At the turn of the last century, the third major marketing and communications breakthrough was taking shape - the telephone. Anyone who answers a telemarketing call now, and is annoyed by it, can hardly imagine how great a breakthrough the telephone was for the people and businesses of its early years. The unwieldy and slow Morse code of the telegraph could now be replaced by the spoken word.

THE AUTOMOBILE AND TRANSPORTATION

Around this same time, in 1908, Henry Ford created the first mass-produced automobile, the Model T, which made transportation more affordable, faster and far more flexible. While Ford's Model T was far from the first automobile produced, it was perhaps the most important automobile ever produced because it was affordable to a much larger part of the population. The combination of the telephone and an affordable automobile ushered in a whole new scale of marketing, on which the smart marketers of today still rely.

During the first half of the 20th century the telephone and the automobile, in combination with the printed word in the form of newspapers and magazines, were joined by yet another new invention, the radio. This combination truly revolutionized marketing again. For the first time ever, large, widespread groups of people were economically accessible to marketing communications. This fact led to the development of larger "stores" and the concept of mass merchandising was born.

The combination of the United States Post Office (founded in 1913), the telephone, railroads, and the automobile (in the form of trucks) permitted early retailing pioneers like Sears, Roebuck (1886) and Montgomery Ward (1872) to build their catalog-mail-order businesses on a much broader scale. Their catalogs were among the most effective and legendary marketing tools ever created.

Remnants of this era remain today as specialty catalogs and are now being replicated digitally on the World Wide Web. As highways were built and transportation improved further, larger retail stores - first for groceries and later for general merchandise - began to spring up in urban and suburban areas of major cities.

TELEVISION AND THE "GOLDEN AGE" OF MARKETING

Concurrent with this infrastructure development was the next great leap in marketing, the development and rapid spread of television. Advertisers everywhere now depend on television so heavily that imagining an era without it is hard to do. Television made it possible to animate the catalogs, to merge the spoken word of radio with the animated pictures and creativity of advertising. Many would say that the hey-day of television, essentially the last half of the twentieth century, was the "golden age" of marketing. If that is so, then a smart marketer would call this the "platinum age," because never before has so much been possible in the form of media tools for the marketer.

> "Just as surely as the Industrial Revolution invaded every sector of society in the 18th and 19th centuries, the e-revolution is creating changes so pervasive and profound that they have the potential of invading every avenue of life in the 21st century. Yet, the more things change, the more they stay the same."
>
> *Blackwell, R.D. and Stephan, K. (July 2000) "The Retail Paradigm." Retail Merchandiser.*

Since most of you were born in the current era, this little history lesson may be a bit old-fashioned and academic, but I went into it because there are important lessons to be learned from history. There's an old saying, "What goes around comes around." It's true! History does tend to repeat itself, with some adaptation to current conditions. The refined version of the Internet that fills the popular news media is less than a decade old.

THE WORLD WIDE WEB

The Mosaic browser, which evolved into Netscape Navigator in 1994, made the World Wide Web a tool for the masses - and for marketing's new era. Connections and communication on the Internet exploded in the period from 1995–2000, and continue to grow. With this came the rapid growth of marketing via the Internet. Only the 2000–2001 collapse of hundreds of prematurely founded and hastily launched (but liberally funded!) dot-coms has caused a pause in the growth of marketing via the Internet. It will resume - count on it.

Every time you read about the incredible revolution that the Internet has made possible, just remember that those previous revolutions such as the invention of the printing press, the telegraph, the telephone, and television had similarly huge impacts on society - and on marketing. Each successive advancement in the speed and reach of communications through the history of man has moved marketing to a new level. The Internet is just doing it again. A wise marketing executive gleans what s/he can from the lessons of the past and avoids the marketing mistakes of a prior era. In doing so, the basis is formed for better marketing decisions in the future.

The need for better, faster decisions is the one aspect of the speed and reach of the Internet era that surpasses the prior upheavals - the speed and reach of the Internet are unprecedented. Nothing in our human experience compares to the blinding, instantaneous, asynchronous, global speed and reach of the Internet. What that means to you is that you have far less time than ever before to make decisions, launch a marketing plan, develop and sell a product or service, and make some money at it before a competitor half way around the world beats you to it. But if you do it well, the entire earth can be your market, faster than ever. How exciting!

GLOBALIZATION AND MASS CUSTOMIZATION

As if the potential for spanning the globe isn't impressive enough, the Internet provides the potential for mass customization. Marketers have always dreamed of the ability to reach out and touch individual customers with their message and their products/services. In the era of mass merchandising, mass media was a sufficient and effective way of marketing. Market research could deal with averages aggregating demand and preferences with only occasional large errors. It's not that way anymore.

The challenge now is that you *can* reach out and touch individual customers. But how? And who? And to do what? Time's up! That's about how long you have to decide! While you were reading the last two sentences some competitor was beating you to the customer. Scary? You bet! Exciting? Absolutely! Marketing in this era is infinitely more fascinating and powerful than in any prior period of time, and the time you need to know about it is *right now*!

There's one more topic I want to touch on briefly before moving on to a whole different set of issues. If I can take you back to the early part of our travel through time, I commented there on the brand the craftsman used to mark his work. Throughout the evolution of marketing from a local, craft-based effort to today's lightning-fast global Internet marketing, brands continue to be one of the most important assets of a marketer. A brand is a shorthand description of a complex package of value, which has made an impression on the mind of the consumer. There's no telling how valuable that impression can be.

> A powerful brand frequently provides the source of a company's wealth for many generations. The best brands improve with age, developing clearly defined personalities, as well as the affection and loyalty of the public. The best become parents to sub-brands and brand extensions, which give the owner a chance to exploit their values and names in new areas.
>
> *Interbrand Group plc (1997) The World's Greatest Brands, New York University Press*

Many brands were built over decades - names like Coke, Marlboro, Mercedes-Benz, AT & T and so forth. Some brands were created more recently. Now familiar names like eBay, Nike, Lexus, Yahoo!, eBay, Cisco, Intel and Microsoft are all products of the past 25 years or less. The Internet and its explosion on the World Wide Web in the last ten years have permitted brand building with unprecedented speed and on a previously unimaginable scale.

America Online (aol.com), Yahoo.com, amazon.com, e-Bay.com and many others were unknown, unheard of and, in many cases, nonexistent 10 years ago. They're almost household names today and the "picture of the package of value that they form in consumers' minds" is extremely valuable in itself. Every marketer must understand brands and brand building - but then I wrote a whole book entitled *Smart Things to Know about Brands and Branding* devoted to that topic - so I will only touch on it in this book where it is an important part of the overall marketing topic.

KEY MILESTONE EVENTS IN MARKETING 1400–1800

- 1411: Mass produced paper - from flour in a German mill.
- 1455: The printing press and movable type - Johann Gutenberg.
- 1825: Railroads - Stockton and Darlington Railway, England, 1825; B. & O., USA, 1828.
- 1844: Telegraph - Samuel Morse, 1844.

- 1860: Pony Express - USA, 1860.
- 1876: Telephones - Alexander Graham Bell, 1876.
- 1885: Automobiles - Karl Benz and Gottlieb Daimler, 1885-6.
- 1886: Mail Order Retailing - US, Montgomery Ward, 1872 and Sears Roebuck, 1886.
- 1913: United States Post Office - USA, 1913.
- 1936: Television - BBC, England, 1936.
- 1950: Marketing's "Golden Age of Television"-1950-2000.
- 1994: Mosaic Web Browsers - Mark Andreesen, Champaign, IL, USA (University of Illinois) 1994.

04

The E-Dimension

This chapter looks at the impact of technological change on marketing by describing many of the new marketing variations introduced by the e-dimension.

THE INTERNET EXPLOSION

The Internet exploded onto the scene as a marketing tool in 1995 with the development of the World Wide Web and the first widely used, consumer friendly Web browser, the Netscape Navigator. The development of search engines that cataloged the rapidly growing number of Websites and pages further enhanced the use of the Internet as a medium for marketing and commerce. Early search sites such as Lycos, Yahoo!, Infoseek, Excite and many others provided, for the first time, a way that potential buyers and sellers could reasonably find each other to do business. In this process a whole new dimension of marketing was born - the "e-dimension."

As companies, individuals and e-entrepreneurs saw the speed, reach and power of this new medium, there was a veritable gold rush of new marketing ideas. These ideas were often exciting, frequently revolutionary, but not always profitable. The hallmark of the early stage of the e-dimension in marketing was much like what occurs in all markets in their infancy. Rapid expansion, numerous new entrants, an almost euphoric sense of the potential, followed by consolidation, shakeout and the inevitable failure of many new entrants. Thus the era of e-commerce was born and suffered through the birthing pains of all new markets.

From this process, many new marketing concepts evolved. A term for selling against (or around) your customers, "Channel conflict," took on new meaning as many companies flocked to the lure of direct internet selling, just because they could - it was the fashionable thing to do. Marketing plans, long the stalwart approach to making sure all the bases were covered, became passé for a while. Then the inadequate plans and impractical methods were exposed for just that by that ultimate "truth-teller," the marketplace. Old marketing ideas, previously either impossible or impractical, were now hot properties - at least for a while.

Forecasts of growth were astronomical, as were the stock market valuations of these new e-companies, until reality struck. The losers with poor or no plans and a weak premise for existence were rapidly eliminated. Millions of dollars were burned in creative advertising for programs, products and companies that would never make it. (Anybody want to buy a sock puppet of a dog that became a famous icon?)

"In the end, this [the Internet] will probably be like the telephone ... this huge new revolution that didn't make much difference to existing social structures."

Steve Woolgar

Then the viable ideas began to emerge. There is real and powerful marketing potential in the Internet world. The problem is that the mixture of the ridiculous and the sublime get blended indiscriminately. What were the major breakthroughs of marketing in the early stage of the e-dimension? What are some of the likely misfires? Good ideas and bad ones are only a hair's breadth apart. The best way to understand that is to understand some of them.

To that end, I will list a couple of dozen of the most common terms and ideas of the e-dimension, and close with two useful perspectives – the stages that all new developments go through, and an example of a good e-dimension partnership.

» *Auctions*: One of the applications which has proven to be a natural for the Internet marketing world is the auction or its derivative, interactive "classified ads." While there are still issues of security and fraud regarding payment and delivery of the authentic item offered, the Internet auction appears to be here to stay. The World Wide Web provides a unique method of matching buyers and sellers and "bidding" on items. www.eBay.com is arguably the dominant Internet auction site. Paypal has also improved the on-line payment process measurably.

Another form of auction which has become a stalwart of the Internet, and which dramatically impacts on industrial marketing, is the business to business (B2B) exchange/marketplace. These sites provide transparent pricing and availability on an immense variety of items for almost every industry. Like the entire Internet syndrome, auctions will go through the normal shakeout, but in the process the transparency of prices and deals will also cause a supplier shakeout – often of epic proportions.

» *Reverse auctions*: If auctions work well on the Internet, then why shouldn't reverse auctions? Actually, they do work pretty well.

www.Priceline.com is one of the pioneers in this form of reverse auction. There is no assurance that the price you offer to pay will be as low as you may find elsewhere, but if it's an OK price, then so be it. Some percentage of Priceline's airline tickets is actually sold at a premium to the prevailing low price because consumers have no idea how low to go. This is a key source of profits for this type of marketing. Some Internet sites are actually selling products at huge premiums to the real value with the promise to rebate 100% of the purchase price 60–90 days later, and after being "requested." Unfortunately for buyers, "later" may turn out to be never, since one of the primary sites doing this is nearly bankrupt. Some attractive marketing models *are* "too good to be true."

» *Shopping "bots*:" The World Wide Web is such a huge shopping place that searching for items is a business in itself. Shopping robots or "bots," typified by sites like www.mySimon.com, travel about visiting Internet Websites and seeking items that users send them looking for. Once the items are found, the site and price are delivered back to the person requesting it. Something similar to this happens in Web-based industrial auctions, too. Bargains are found, but the sheer size and complexity of the Web precludes even the best shopping bots from finding every place items are sold. The same goes for matching industrial buyers and sellers.

» *Portals*: The one-stop place to shop for information and connections: www.aol.com (America Online), www.yahoo.com, and www.msn.com (Microsoft) are just three leading examples. The portal is the doorway to the Web, the ultimate catalog index, and a one-stop place to make your Web surfing experience a little simpler. The result is lots of visitors to portals. This makes portals ripe candidates for advertising on the Web. No one has yet figured out how to value Web advertising, but if getting a lot of people to see an ad - even if fleetingly - creates advertising value, portals get the job done. These companies are among the few that seem to have viable profit models for Internet business, which are heavily based on marketing and service to customers.

» *On-line retailers*: amazon.com is the most well known and "successful" of the Internet retailers - unless earning a profit is part of the definition of success. Profitability is something that eluded amazon.com in its early years, unless it resorted to financial gymnastics. It is finally beginning to generate acceptable financial results. Amazon is a great shopping site. It has wide variety, fast searches, easy ordering, creative marketing tools and good prices. Profits were slow coming, which raised concerns about its long-term survival. Can it survive? Can it really make good money long-term. Probably, if it can continue to enter into the right kind of alliances like the one with Toys R Us (described later). Many traditional retailers have flocked to the Internet, and many specialty retailers remain in business although the dropouts outnumber the survivors about ten to one. Internet retailers are somewhat like catalog retailers, and that has never been a highly profitable form of retailing except for those retailers who serve the "niches with the riches" - high end specialty products with good profit margins, modest assortment and relatively low delivery cost.

» *Internet chat groups*: Word of mouth never had it so good. This isn't a marketing topic - or is it? Ever heard of the Motley Fool? In the early years of AOL, this site was as close to an on-line investment services marketing site as they came. Of course the price was "free" and the services were risky (investment advice), but when you don't pay anything, it is "*Caveat emptor*" (let the buyer beware). Chat groups are bigger than ever, and anyone who figures out how to do viral marketing through them will reap a large reward in potential customers. Until then, chat groups are the modern Internet equivalent to the old telephone party line.

» *On-line investing*: www.etrade.com, www.eschwab.com, www.ameritrade.com and many others broke into the market and showed millions how to lose money faster than ever by doing their own on-line investing. One of the hottest areas of the dot-com boom in 2000 was the explosion of on-line stock trading services. More money was lost in this way than in any other legal investment scheme. The Internet made it so simple to trade stocks. The boom made it so easy for an investor to think s/he was a real "maven." Wrong! The main marketing value of on-line trading was that it made advertising agencies and media a lot of money, and dramatically reduced the transaction prices of conventional brokerages. Once again, as in most of the e-dimension cases, pricing transparency depressed prices dramatically and forced an entire industry to restructure to survive.

» *E-cash and E-stamps*: These are two ideas whose times will come, just not yet. Just as industrial marketers were afraid to assign mission critical functions to an erratic, insecure Internet (they stayed with private EDI systems), so are individuals wary of sending their precious funds through cyberspace. Stamps are just another form of currency, and one with very limited use. Until the postal services find a way to provide more flexible access to using services like www.estamps.com, conventional stamps, like conventional banks and stockbrokers, will prevail. But, when the dam breaks, get ready to run - because there will be a veritable flood of users and uses of e-cash and e-stamps, e-credit, and more.

» *Permission marketing*: This term was mentioned earlier and was created in a book by former Yahoo! marketing guru Set Godin. It is a good, entertaining book. Most marketing requires one of two things to happen: either the customer voluntarily comes to a place where marketing is done and they expect it; or they are interrupted in the process of doing something else by an intrusive message. Although the intrusion is usually tolerated, more and more consumers are finding ways (or governments are passing laws), to limit the extent of the intrusion. Godin's premise is that marketing is based on a relationship and the best possible one is when the prospect grants "permission" to be the target of a marketing effort. One of his best examples of this is a subscription. A subscription is just such an extended form of permission marketing, and done properly is a means of both sustaining the relationship and creating an annuity of continuing business.

» *WebBlogs*: This is a new web phenomenon that is exploding in growth. "Blogs" are sites where individuals can post their thoughts on almost any topic for everyone to read-and respond-if they wish. Estimates vary, but upwards of 15 million "blog" sites probably exist and more are being added each day. Using blogs as marketing tools is a logical and likely development, but as yet, no firm direction has emerged.

» *Spam*: It is impossible to stop a major new form of "junk mail" - at least so far it is. Spam is perhaps the most undesirable marketing side effect of the Web. It is both a marketing tool and the bane of a marketer's existence. Like "junk mail," Spam comes whether the recipient wants it or not. It is neither desirable nor attractive in most cases. Junk mail is expensive to produce, send and deliver (and dispose of). Spam is none of these. Buy a list of e-mail addresses, and broadcast away, at very minimal cost. The cost is borne by the recipients who must clear this electronic junk mail from mailboxes and servers. Thus far, no effective form of control has been devised. Marketing by direct e-mail can be tremendously powerful and inexpensive, but its success will be limited as long as Spam remains uncontrollable - because it is too hard to tell the difference between good marketing contacts and Spam.

» *Banner ads*: These flashing, blinking, scrolling and crawling visual interruptions catch the attention of more Web surfers than critics claim, but are of dubious value. The click through rate is lower than junk mail responses, and the cost is all over the map. Perhaps there is value in launching unknown brands in that manner, but there is also risk. Any advertising method that is essentially annoying and pervasive can generate as much ill will as good will. Unlike some advertising people who claim that any impression is valuable, I disagree. Good impressions are valuable. Bad ones are not.

» *Pop-up/pop-under windows*: These raise intrusiveness to a new level and, unlike banners, cannot be ignored. The Web surfer must consciously click a box to make them go away. While they can carry useful information and be extremely functional at times, they must be used with discretion or they just become another annoyance. A new generation of pop-up blocking software promises to substantially reduce the usefulness of that annoying marketing method.

» *Identity Theft & Phishing*: These terms describe two of the most dangerous aspects of the Internet's evolution. Massive identity theft has already occurred, but fortunately, little of it has been used for major criminal purposes. This does not mean that criminals won't use stolen identities for illicit purposes. Such activities undermine the security of Internet transactions and do untold harm to on-line marketing and sales efforts. "Phishing" is a subset of identity theft. The term describes a deceptive practice that maliciously misleads a web user into providing private/personal information by submitting it to legitimate-looking copies of reputable web sites. Often victims of phishing do not even know they have been victimized. I call it "maliciously misleading marketing." Unfortunately, each new media gives rise to new forms of crime, and these are two of the most potentially harmful.

» *Pornography*: The Web is the ultimate dirty picture book/video. Some say the only truly profitable business on the Web is pornography. They may be right, because it is a very large business indeed. Good marketers avoid these kinds of methods, unless that is the business they are in. Then they have a different problem and it is a moral one, not a business problem.
» *Global market aggregation*: One of the most exciting aspects of marketing in the e-dimension is that a company can aggregate markets and communities in ways never before possible. The reach and speed of the Web makes it possible to find common interests so diverse that no conventional marketing approach could ever reach them all - at least not economically. Now marketing is truly global in this respect - at least wherever the Internet reaches.
» *B2C*: The early acronym for Business-to-Consumer selling. Much the same comments apply to this as to Web retailing. The idea is great, the information component is rich, the speed spectacular and the front-end part is easy. But someone must still do the other stuff - pricing, forecasting, sourcing, production, fulfillment and distribution. These costs are largely about the same, Web or no Web. None the less, the aggregating ability of the Web is powerful and and surviving B2C companies like amazon.com are now growing in size and profitability.
» *B2B*: The shorthand term for Business-to-Business commerce. The Web is coming along in this area, but the hope has not yet matched the hype. As with auctions, many B2B marketplace exchanges are passing events as buyers wring the last drop of inefficiency and windfall profits out of suppliers. Then what will happen? The huge auto industry B2B exchange is called Covisint. Will it be successful? Sure, it will squeeze already weak suppliers harder yet, but in the long run the strong will survive and the weak will drop. Savings in transaction costs due to electronics will be attractive at first. Later,

the suppliers will figure out whom they want to do business with, and exchanges will not alter that decision.

The buyers - huge powerful companies - don't really want the same deals from the same group of suppliers. Each of these behemoths wants their own best deal, and that will ultimately undermine Covisint. The same challenge faces B2B exchanges. Only those that serve a wide industry group in a non-competing fashion are likely to flourish (e.g., sites that provide freight tracking services for many freight companies). While this shakeout occurs, you must market to them; capitalize on them; and hang on until they prove or disprove their long-term viability.

» *CRM*: Shorthand for Customer Relationship Management, which is a systems based formalization of the processes, transactions and information repositories all companies accumulate about their customers, but are otherwise unable to aggregate, sort, access and use. This is a powerful new way to improve customer service by using the power of technology to complement the value of relationships.
» *Knowledge repositories/data warehouses*: These are one of the key features that led to CRM, and help make true the saying, "If we only knew what we already know, we'd be much more effective at serving our customers."[2] These actually go far beyond customer knowledge to encompass competitive information, market information, product information, and any other form of stored knowledge that a company wants to make accessible and easily shared.
» *On-line collateral materials*: One of the key features of intranets and Internet technology is the decline/demise of the expensive and rapidly obsolete supplies of expensive paper catalogs, price lists, spec sheets, and related collateral materials. Now this information can all be placed on the Web, in digital format, and printed on demand. Only when companies need the superb reproduction quality and/or the tactile benefit of a binder, heavy paper, shiny photos and/or durable catalogs will they resort to old lithographic or offset printed information. Paper will not go away! But the amount of obsolete paper to pitch and write off should go down massively.
» *MP3, Napster and Gnutella*: Since the Web is essentially a huge number of interconnected computers, it was inevitable that someone

would devise a way to digitize music (MP3) or videos and someone else would find a way to share them free of charge (Napster and Gnutella ... and a raft of others). Just as the Xerox machine made a travesty of some print copyright laws, these Web-based forms of copying, sharing (pirating?) and distributing entertainment media are deconstructing and revolutionizing the recorded entertainment industry - the hard way! How it all shakes out will depend on court decisions and/or the music companies figuring out what it really is they have to sell. Apple Computer's iPod and iTunes not only facilitated the legal sale of digital music, it also gave birth to yet another new phenomenon-"pod-casts"-an as yet unexploited, but potentially powerful marketing media format.

» *Internet telephony*: VoIP is the new acronym. Standing for "Voice over Internet Protocol," this takes the use of the Internet as a communications medium in yet another way. Telemarketers may have an even greater field day if they can not only send printed material (Spam), but also make the equivalent of annoying telephone calls to computers all over the world. This technology is still coming of age, but it has already depressed long distance telephone rates, and there is more room for them to drop. Then comes the challenge of appropriating the bandwidth needed to support these new protocols. VoIP pioneers like Vonage and Skype have opened a "Brave New World" for global telephony, marketing and communications.
» *Broadband & Wi-Fi*: The umbrella term for the variety of transmission systems that carry a huge volume of digital signal traffic, often completely wireless in transmission. Typical of these is the huge bandwidth provided by cable modems, DSL, transmitted over fiber optic or coaxial cables, satellites, etc. Known as "the big pipe," broadband opens new marketing possibilities limited only by the imagination. Voice, pictures, combinations of the two and more can be sent as easily as a simple e-mail. The challenge for marketers is what to do with this power, and how to use it effectively. Wi-Fi's explosive spread offers an entirely new marketing media format with the ability to reach anyone, anywhere, anytime once these pervasive wireless networks are completed-connecting computers, cell phones and PDAs of all kinds.

> "The ability to communicate readily, at great distances, is embodied only in angels. Distance is a fundamental premise of a material world. It fell not to the telegraph, the telephone, the television, or the airplane. None of these achieve true action at a distance. Transmitting a few words, a few minutes of voice, even the few filmed spectacles that broadcasters deign to bounce around the globe, serves only to remind us how bound and gagged we are . . . These gags and ties are now giving way. When anyone can transmit any amount of information, any picture, any experience, any opportunity to anyone, or everyone anywhere at any time, instantaneously, without barriers of convenience or cost, the resulting transformation becomes a transfiguration."
>
> *George Gilder, Gilder Technology Report 2000*

- *e-Advertising*: Banners, Spam, pop-up windows, inserts, etc., etc., *ad infinitum*. All appear on your e-mail and Web browser. What's it worth? How to measure it? What to do with it? Marketing's job is to understand the power of the media and then use it to convey and communicate with customers and prospects the merits of their products or services. Getting feedback is easier than ever. Knowing what to do with it isn't. The medium is not the message, but the medium influences the message in both quality and cost-effectiveness.
- *e-Brands and e-everything*: A decade ago, no one would believe that brands like eBay, amazon, Yahoo! or AOL could be built into household names to rival Coke, Marlboro, in five years or less. Some brands grew like weeds and wilted just as fast. Others are destined to become great long-term brands. The ability to build brands faster than ever is the key point. The reach and speed of the Internet redefines what marketing can do, and establishes new rules for what it must do. Simply throwing money at advertising is not building a brand. A brand is both a promise (of value) and a relationship (based on trust). It's one thing to advertise it. It's entirely another to offer the value proposition and *sustain it*.

Compare AOL to Prodigy or CompuServe and you can recognize the difference.

RULES FOR SUCCESS IN E-BUSINESS[3]

1 To be successful in e-business you have to be in e-business.
2 Make your CEO your Internet evangelist. Make him or her responsible for your e-commerce success.
3 Give everyone access to everything all the time. You need a Freedom of Information Act for corporate data.
4 Train and motivate your customers and employees to always go to the Web.

The next stage of the e-dimension will be a real revolution based on learning from and the new application of improvements based on past (painful) experience. The key knowledge is how to survive the "Five stages of the revolution." To know that, you must first recognize what they are, then plan for what to do. Here are the stages and some actions for survival.

FIVE STAGES OF THE REVOLUTION

» *Experimentation*: Be persistent, flexible, and very willing to experiment. (But manage your losses, and don't fall in love with your own ideas unless lots of customers do!)
» *Capitalization*: Have vision, connections, skillful salesmanship, and a source of good advice. (Cash is like oxygen. Without it you die. Get plenty and manage it accordingly.)
» *Management*: Cultivate experience, teamwork, motivation, and an obsession with detail. (But don't let postponed perfection get in the way of planned progress. Do something then correct the mistakes and move ahead.)
» *Hyper-competition*: This is the really tough stage! Getting through it is critical. You must have "deep pockets" (cash). You must also be paranoid, responsive and market like hell. (And when you finish that, "leap a couple of tall buildings in a single bound" just to stay in training - that will be what it takes.)

» *Consolidation*: Become a dealmaker, negotiator, and public relations flack - and hire good lawyers. (If you have a choice, don't be one of the "consolidatees," try to be one of the "consolidators" - even if you have to start small! The management in them is less likely to get downsized out onto the street.)

AN IMPORTANT MESSAGE – REVISITED!

"Over the course of a few years, a new communications technology annihilated distance and shrank the world faster and further than ever before. A world-wide communications network whose cables spanned continents and oceans, it revolutionized business practices and gave rise to new forms of crime."

Steve Woolgar - talking about the telegraph in 1840 - not the Internet

TOYS R US AND AMAZON.COM – A MARKETING PARTNERSHIP THAT SHOULD HAVE WORKED

Amazon.com's partnership with toy retailer Toys R Us (TRU) was the prototype for the partnership of an old economy and new economy company. Amazon.com broke a new frontier in B2C (Business to Consumer) with its pioneering work as a bookseller. The problem was that amazon.com kept spending ahead of its sales and was slow in making a profit despite its rapid growth. There are those, author included, who question whether amazon's original model could work at all in the long term.

However, a partnership between an experienced and established "bricks and mortar" company and amazon was a good one. TRU attempted to launch its own Web initiative twice - once on its own and once in a partnership with Benchmark Partners. Each failed because it (and its management and board) could not come to grips with the issue of cannibalizing its own retail store sales.

The problem with the toy business is that it is seasonal and volatile. Missed sales at Christmas due to stock-outs end up being lost sales. Guess wrong on the inventory, and there is big trouble.

Meanwhile, in the early dot-com explosion, e-Toys and Toysmart.com were getting all the publicity, the media hype, and a concerning amount of online sales. Yet neither of these two had the economic staying power nor the long-term business potential a TRU – amazon partnership provided.

So, while TRU struggled with its Web presence, amazon struggled with its fulfillment costs and inventory management. E-Toys and Toysmart.com struggled just to exist. When amazon.com and TRU joined forces in a partnership, a strong new model was born. Amazon.com provided the front end – taking orders and handling the transaction from the Web information technology side. TRU, with its network of retail stores and large sales base, provided the inventory cushion and fulfillment through existing distribution centers (those of either amazon or TRU).

Disney quickly grabbed Toysmart.com but the combination was not the right cultural chemistry. Disney's tradition-bound, large company mentality was diametrically opposed to Toysmart.com's fast and loose approach to the business. When Disney attempted to conserve Toysmart.com's dwindling cash by insisting that it concentrate its advertising on Disney's ABC television, Toysmart.com resisted. Finally, while the two tugged back and forth, the cash ran out.

As amazon.com and TRU joined forces, the toy business that naturally flowed through this powerful combination of the premier global toy retailer and the premier Web retailer drained valuable volume from remaining dot-com toy retailer e-Toys. E-toys had a bit more staying power than Toysmart.com, but it just ran out of cash in the 2001 post-Christmas sales doldrums. A vast percentage of toy business is done in the fourth quarter of the year. Without any additional revenue to sustain it through the slower parts of the year, e-toys is gone, and its inventory and customer list divided like spoils among new and old-economy merchants.

The best partnerships are win-win, and use the relative strengths of each partner to make up for the other partner's weaknesses. That is exactly what should have happened in this case. It was a model that amazon was to use again and again. Only when the partners become selfish, do such partnerships turn from win-win to lose-lose. In this one, both partners lost. It should have worked.

NOTES

1 Kranhold, K. (June 27, 2000) ''Web Sites Toot Their Horns Amid Ad Chill.'' *The Wall Street Journal*.
2 Quoted from Jim Hawley, Business Unit Manager, Manco, Inc.
3 Friedman, T. (2000) *The Lexus and the Olive Tree*. Anchor Books, New York (quoting Alan Cohen of Cisco).

The Global Dimension

The global aspects of marketing are discussed in this chapter. Global marketing development is proceeding rapidly and this chapter illustrates how to deal with it by "thinking global, yet acting local."

THE SHRINKING WORLD

The world is a shrinking place. Distances are diminishing faster than ever. Information travels around the world in an instant. People can be anywhere in a day. Work goes on around the clock, around the globe. The global village of television is now more extensive than ever. As more and more people can see what they might have, and have what they might want, and make what they might be able to sell, the entire process of marketing is turned into a more important, more complex opportunity than ever before. No one knows who makes what they think are familiar brands. Sony, Nike, Apple, Volkswagen . . . who makes what, where? Who knows? Who cares? Marketers should, and here's why.

If you recall the history of marketing evolution, competition in the olden days was a decidedly local phenomenon. Craftsmen only had to compete with other craftsmen within a limited distance of where they were located. As transportation and communication methods grew, the corresponding area of competition grew with them. What was once local became regional; what was regional became national and now, what was national has quickly become global competition.

The people of less developed countries (LDCs) are anxious and hungry for a better standard of living. Thus they will work for much lower wages. This has a profound effect on the costs of products, which in turn influence the prices expected by the markets. And that has changed marketing more than anyone could imagine.

Typically products and technology developments have come from older and wealthier areas of the world. Europe has been (and still is) the source of much of the world's innovation. As Europeans emigrated to what is now the United States, and early European traders settled in coastal areas around the world (Hong Kong/China, New York/US, Australia, etc.) these areas became the seats of knowledge, commerce and innovation. But a few decades ago, the use of telephones, jet aircraft, fax machines and, recently, the Internet, accelerated the transfer of technology around the world.

GLOBAL COMPETITION

As Thomas Friedman so ably describes in his book *The Lexus and the Olive Tree*, globalization is here to stay and it has changed life and business in the world forever. The major companies of the world - Coca-Cola, McDonald's, GM, Ford, Gillette, 3M, LVMH, Vivendi, DaimlerChrylser, Sony, Matsushita, Toyota, Honda, Samsung and so many more are now multi-national companies and global competitors. There are literally hundreds, maybe thousands, of invisible global competitors, mostly from LDCs and without world-known brands - for now.

Look at any durable branded product you can find. The odds are good that it was made in China, Malaysia, Taiwan, Korea, or some more remote country around the globe. Check the labels on clothing and you will see a different list - Malaysia, Indonesia, Philippines, Haiti, Dominican Republic, and Mexico - once again, all LDCs, or at least low labor cost countries.

Much of the software used today is written in India while those in the Western hemisphere are sleeping. The package doesn't carry that information, but check it out and you will find it to be true.

As competition has globalized, another phenomenon has occurred. There is latent global over-capacity for almost everything, if one looks for it. The retailing behemoths, Wal*Mart, Carrefour, Tesco, and others *do* look for it. Marketers need to learn not only to look for it, but to know where competition is likely to come from.

There are two sides to the marketing coin in an era of globalization. Where will the product be sold, and where will it be made? Marketing needs to carefully understand the implications of both. Costs vary. Cultures vary. Retail methods vary, influencing packaging and merchandising. Communications and entertainment vary and influence advertising and promotion. Pricing strategies must consider local competition and global sourcing as well as the cost of global logistics.

If this all sounds complicated, it is. But it is the real world for marketers in the twenty-first century. What globalization has done is open a veritable Pandora's box of opportunities and threats. Marketers must sort out these opportunities to capitalize on the best and reject the rest. They must then factor in the threats and avoid the pitfalls of coming to market with too little, too late.

How to do this? Get help. There are companies that support global marketing efforts, multi-national branding and advertising and international sourcing. Form a partnership, an alliance or a coalition of people and organizations who know the conditions in the global markets where products and services are being bought, sold and delivered. Only by taking this comprehensive approach can marketers avoid the traps so often encountered. World leaders have learned from their mistakes. P & G initially introduced laundry products to China in packages that were much too large; then they learned and changed to single use or smaller packets. US retailers like Toys R Us entered global markets early and learned that the cultures and toys were not quite the same around the world; then they adjusted. Office products popular in the US for storing and queuing paper in cubicles are useless in Japan where cubicles don't exist and storing or queuing paper is considered the height of inefficiency. Even language nuances can be an obstacle, as GM found when its car named Nova (in the US) was launched in a country were *"no va"* means "won't go" - not the best name for a car.

Are these old examples silly? Sure they are - but they really happened and weren't silly to the marketers who made these mistakes.

COUNTERFEITS TELL A LOT ABOUT GLOBAL DEVELOPMENT

One of my resources told me a story I'll never forget. The essence of it was this. As countries around the globe develop in competence, one of the stages they all go through is the production of counterfeit goods. Even the US went through this stage, but in an earlier century. A clear tip off about how developed the country is can be found by their relative counterfeiting status.

Take the ubiquitous Rolex watch knock off. In early stages of industrial development, countries learn to make relatively poor but tolerable copies of prestige items like a classic Rolex watch. Other commonly counterfeited items are Louis Vuitton luggage, Gucci purses, Hermès scarves, Burberry accessories, and lately, Nike sportswear.

When a country like Vietnam is in rather early developmental stages, the Rolex watches are OK (the electronic movements from Japan work fine), but the workmanship is poor and the price is low - US$10. As the markets advance, perhaps to the level of Thailand, the workmanship gets better and the price goes up too - to US$20. More developed industrial markets such as the more advanced areas of China near Hong

Kong can make very nice looking counterfeits, but these sell for more like US$30–40.

Countries like Taiwan and Korea, which were the primary source of such counterfeit watches a decade or more ago, are now making goods so sophisticated that they could make the real thing. If they wanted to invest in the precious metals, then the Rolex brand would be the obstacle, because the price would not be enough cheaper for the "authentic" knock off. Really genuine looking knock offs are available in Hong Kong (and New York City?) for $60 and up!

As the countries of the world develop, the motivation moves from counterfeiting to producing the real article and earning some of the profits that go along with that stage of development. So, if you want to determine the approximate level of global development of a country, check out where it stands on the counterfeiting scale.

> "Companies will need global reach to serve global customers. If they lack the capacity, they must build partnerships around the world. All markets are local markets. Quality, pricing and service must be globally competitive and domestically appropriate. Local distribution will require a much deeper understanding of local business needs and prevailing national cultures."
>
> *Robert Rosen*[1]

GLOBALIZATION OF MASS RETAILING

No book on marketing would be complete without a section on the increasing globalization of retailing. Boutique shops have long found their way to prestigious shopping centers. Prada, Louis Vuitton, Gucci and many others have placed stores in shopping centers from San Francisco to Singapore, Hong Kong to New York. Go into these stores and centers in which they reside, and you are instantly in a familiar setting. Whether it is the World Trade Center in Bangkok, Thailand or the Harborside shopping complex in Kowloon (Hong Kong), China, these boutiques are relatively uniform, and so are the marketing plans behind them. High fashion is a globally uniform market.

What is not so uniform is the other end of the spectrum. Warehouse clubs like Costco and Sam's, office product retailers like Staples and OfficeMax found very different (and hostile) environments as they expanded globally. Toys R Us was one of the pioneer global retailers, expanding from its US base into dozens of countries in the 1980s. Some of its lessons were painful, but it carved out strong positions in most of those markets with its formula of a huge assortment and highly competitive pricing.

The current wave of retailing expansion that is influencing marketing on a global scale is that of general merchandise mass retailing. Wal*Mart, the world's largest retailer (approaching $300bn in sales) is now a factor in many countries, and especially strong in US neighbors Canada and Mexico.

As Wal*Mart moved out of North America, it found that its formula for retail value was still valid, but required "tweaking" to compete. This "tweaking" meant that the suppliers who served Wal*Mart had to make some major changes in their own marketing plans for those countries.

WAL*MART LEARNS THE HARD WAY

In Mexico, one of Wal*Mart's early entries, it partnered with Mexican retailer Cifra and learned that it must use multiple formats to reach the Mexican markets. Wal*Mart currently uses five different formats in the Mexican market:

- Superama - an upscale supermarket that rivals the best of US operations;
- Aurrera - the original large footprint super-center style stores;
- Bodega - a smaller version of the Aurrera format that is a low-cost operation targeted to the very value-conscious shopper;
- Suburbia - a mid-tier department store format;
- VIPs - a chain of over 300 quick service restaurants.

Clearly Wal*Mart learned from Cifra that a one-size fits all format would not maximize its success in Mexico. The marketers at Wal*Mart's supplier companies would be well advised to realize this as well. Then, if emerging markets follow the trends in the US market, Wal*Mart (and its suppliers) will force the retailers already in the market to do something different to compete – and this too will force marketers at their suppliers to react as well.

Some of the practices used in international stores, like the presentation and assortment of seafood, are being transplanted into Wal*Mart's US super-centers. Formats like Bodega worked well enough to transplant into Brazil, but the name didn't translate well, so those stores will now be called "Todo Dia."

Marketers would do well to notice the challenges faced by Wal*Mart in its global expansion, since these are much the same as most global expansions will encounter. As international consultant John Anderson puts it, "Doing business abroad means doing about 80% of the same things as you do anywhere, but you'd better understand the 20% that needs to be different if you want to succeed."

Wal*Mart ran into entrenched competition in Brazil. Global retail giant Carrefour had been there since the 1970s, and it has a store base today of 74 hypermarkets and 115 supermarkets. It was not going to roll over for Wal*Mart.

Neither was the number two retailer, a homegrown firm named Companhia Brasileira de Distribuicao (CBD). CBD grew its store base to over 400 by 2000, and used a variety of formats to do so in spite of Wal*Mart's market entry. Extra Hipermercados and two other supermarket formats went after different segments of that market. Pao de Acucar goes after upper-income customers, and Barateiro Supermercados goes after the other end with a no-frills format using private-label goods. Electro is CBD's home appliance and electronics store format.

Korea's dense population (half of the country's population is in Seoul) and high real estate costs dictated that Wal*Mart use a multi-storey store format, far different from its footprint in most other markets. Here too it had to cope with the competitive entry a year earlier of Carrefour and in the same year of British retailer Tesco.

Clearly Wal*Mart has learned to "think global" and "act local" and it learned the hard way – through experience.

China's 1.3 billion people is too attractive a market to overlook, but the low income of the people dictates widely differing retailing and product choices. Smaller packages, for more frequent smaller purchases, seem to be a common theme. It can take Chinese customers five visits to store to purchase as much as a single US retail shopper buys. This means more congested stores and different merchandising methods are needed.

US retailer J.C. Penney bought control of a Brazilian department store, Lojas Renner (Porto Allegre, Brazil) and has built it into a 49-store mini-success story. After failures in Chile, Indonesia and the Philippines, J.C. Penney learned something. It retained local store names and most of the store management. The focus for the parent was on back-room operations and some merchandise presentation concepts. After the failure of two other large Brazilian department store chains, Renner has grown nicely and is expanding to larger city markets.

The message for marketers is this. While brands may be global and need to stay that way, the method of going to market may be as similar as the pricey designer stores or as different as the mass retailing/department store segments. Understanding the local market, local competition and local preferences is a global marketing imperative. The overused phrase "think global, act local" is an apt one.

BRANDING MUST BE CONSISTENT

A glance at the dazzling Hong Kong skyline at night makes this point all too well. Brands are global. The major brand names shown there in lighted signs are a multi-national who's who of product companies, airlines, financial services firms and much more. A glimpse at New York's Times Square district or Tokyo's Ginza echoes the same message.

Global brand names transcend language differences. Sony, Coke, Marlboro, Samsung, Nike, McDonald's, BMW, and Louis Vuitton are all names and brands known worldwide. This global uniformity dictates that, as much as marketers must tailor presentation to the local needs, the brand must retain its uniform image and identity. Packages may require different languages - three, four or even six languages on some European products - but the brand and its icon, name and/or symbol must retain its consistent visual identity regardless of where in the world it is seen.

CONSOLIDATION IS A GLOBAL ISSUE

The last point to make about marketing and globalization is that companies continue to consolidate globally more aggressively than ever. Vivendi-Universal has become an entertainment colossus, as has AOL-Time-Warner. DaimlerChrysler now owns those brands and a large stake in Mitsubishi; Ford owns Jaguar and Volvo. GM owns Saab as well as lesser stakes in smaller Japanese makers. Advertising agencies, banks, brokerages, and companies in many other industries are being consolidated as weaker, smaller competitors are bought, merged and rationalized into larger and larger global entities.

Whether this scale makes them more powerful or more like dinosaurs of eons past is arguable. Consumers care less about who owns the brand and the product/service than what kind of value it offers, and how well it lives up to its brand promise. Brands are shorthand for packages of value; brands are promises and relationships. Don't ever betray them or let them fall apart, because it won't matter what global corporate entity was at fault - the brand will suffer.

There are few things more powerful and valuable in an era of global marketing than strong, well-known and respected brands. Pricing has become increasingly transparent aided by the omni-present Internet. Consumers are more in control than ever. Whether it is in Boston or Beijing, Cairo or Chicago, Nike is still Nike; Sony is still Sony. Study after study has shown that, once consumers find a brand they like and can trust, they keep coming back and buying it over and over. No amount of globalization seems likely to change that fact.

If marketing is about "having what will sell," then having what will sell and the brand to identify it is the key to success in an era of globalization.

NOTE

1 Rosen, R. (2000) *Global Literacies*. Simon & Schuster, New York.

06

The State of the Art

The state of the art of marketing is discussed in this chapter in the form of brief illustrations of leading-edge marketing in use and the principles embodied in each case.

"IF WE ONLY KNEW WHAT WE ALREADY KNOW . . ."

It is hard for employees at large companies to know everything that the "company" knows, and even harder to share that knowledge. As one marketing executive I know puts it, "If we only knew what we already know, we'd be much more effective." US consumer goods company Procter & Gamble is trying to make that come true with a project internally called "Project Enterprise Marketing Management" or "Project m."

Its goal is to reduce the time it takes to develop and market products by making it easier for employees to share knowledge and work together. It is forming a venture with Magnifi, a closely held marketing services firm, to do this. The new, jointly formed company will create software for the P & G computers that will permit employees around the globe to do many jobs faster and better, to collaborate on documents, to watch TV commercials being developed, or to see if an approval needed has been received.

Not only will the programs make much more information available in real time, they will leave a virtual "paper trail" showing who is next on project tasks of approvals, who has completed assigned work, and what is next. This will help pinpoint bottlenecks and assist project newcomers in getting up to speed on where things stand. P & G has 30–50% a personnel turnover of on a given major project during the course of completing the project, so getting new people into the project flow is a critical need.

Another valuable purpose of the project is to capture "corporate memory." As more and more senior people leave the company, a trend that demographics predict will grow in the decade, much useful experience and wisdom is lost. While computers cannot replace the people, they can capture many of the decisions, the basis for them, and the outcomes. Having this information available should help new managers make more intelligent decisions and avoid pitfalls that were known in the past.

If P & G is successful with this initiative, it hopes to invite key suppliers and advertising agencies to sign up as well. As is true for all information, sharing it makes it grow and become a richer resource for everyone to use. This is a new era of marketing, and P & G is experimenting with a powerful new tool for that era.

In the sections that follow I will go "from CRM to Branding and Advertising to Strategy to Globalization to CPFR," which sort of summarizes the current "buzz-words" and acronyms, but also covers the range from getting, keeping and caring for the customer to assuring that the consumer's and customer's needs are fulfilled.

Don't confuse the simplicity of the acronyms with the complexity of the management principles underlying them. I have also included a few relevant examples of how companies are using these and other contemporary marketing concepts to succeed in the toughest business environment this world has ever known.

CRM/PRM

Tools: Customer Relationship Management/Partner Relationship Management

CRM is a popular acronym ("buzz-word") for age-old processes translated to the new computer/web-based economy. Its devotees describe CRM as "the overall process of marketing, sales, and service within any organization." Others say it differently: "a business strategy to get, grow and retain the right customers, leading to long term profitability." As customer service expectations continue to escalate, more companies, especially larger ones, are turning to CRM to help integrate their far-flung dealings with customers.

PRM or Partner Relationship Management is a subset of CRM, and is "the application of Relationship Management strategies and technologies to the unique needs of indirect sales channels." CRM and PRM systems are supposed to help businesses develop and sustain profitable customer/channel partner relationships - and maybe they do. At least the software industry is hoping to sell about $2bn of supporting systems in the next 2–3 years. The good news is the attention being paid to serving customer partners more effectively.

> "Customer Relationship Management (CRM) is a business strategy to select and manage customer relationships to

optimize long-term value to an enterprise. CRM requires a customer-centric business philosophy and culture to support effective marketing, sales and service processes across all direct and indirect customer interaction channels. CRM software applications can enable effective Customer Relationship Management, provided an enterprise has the right strategy, leadership and culture."

www.CRMGuru.com

Companies are investing in CRM in hopes of becoming more effective in their selling while gaining competitive differentiation in a world where pricing is globally transparent and products become commodities overnight. But there is no replacement for good old-fashioned customer relationships - between people! What CRM will do is provide a multi-channel tool for the people to share what is happening and how customer needs and company capabilities can be best matched - and that is a very good thing to do.

Key functional areas of CRM include:

» *Marketing automation* - target the best customers, manage marketing campaigns, generate quality leads, and share the information easily.
» *Sales automation* - support the selling process from lead qualification to closing the business.
» *Customer service* - resolve customer issues after the sale responsively, building customer satisfaction and loyalty.
» *E-commerce* - handle the transaction online, as a seamless extension of the sales process.

Information should flow easily between these functional areas, facilitating collaborative team selling and support. This can be accomplished with CRM suites or by integrating best-of-breed solutions. Increasingly, Internet-based CRM and PRM systems are the norm, providing a common platform to deliver applications for use by employees, partners, and customers.

"As a rule, however, enterprises have re-discovered the importance of channel partners."[1]

Tips for winning with CRM[2]

- *Deliver value first*. Your customers don't care about your management problems. Make sure their experience is one that will motivate them to return again and again, and to make positive referrals.
- *It's still about people*. Technology is great but, without executive leadership, employee and partner buy-in and a genuine emotional bond with your customers, a CRM project won't be successful.
- *Pick CRM partners, not vendors*. Find software and service firms that are as committed to you as you are to your customers. In other words, pick CRM technology partners that practice good Customer Relationship Management.
- *"Ready, fire, aim" doesn't work*. Resist the temptation to make it up as you go. CRM is complex. Use process analysis and planning methodologies to avoid costly and time-consuming rework later on. Installing software means nothing.
- *Treat partners like customers*. You can't do it all alone; get some help! To win the battle for the mind share with indirect sales channels, invest in tools to enable partners to do business more effectively and efficiently.

Marketing lessons from anecdotal evidence abound - consider these examples.

REVOLUTION?

Strategy: "Law Firms, in a Competitive Bid, Appoint Chief Marketing Officers"[3]

Even professions once considered to be above the practice of marketing are now required to be realistic. Competition exists in all endeavors, and especially where companies are vying for the attention and business of consumer customers. Ever since a 1977

US Supreme Court decision legalizing advertising by law firms, some firms have advertised. But most of them were the so-called "ambulance chasers" seeking consumers who could provide them cases with large potential contingency settlements.

Now the prestige firms are getting involved. Orrick, Herrington & Sutcliff, a 575 attorney global firm recently added a chief marketing officer to its key office listing. So, also, have Brobeck, Phleger & Harrison, a 950 attorney firm with headquarters in San Francisco, CA (US), and Pittsburgh, PA (US) firm Kirkpatrick & Lockhart LLP consisting of 630 attorneys.

It seems the litigious US market place has become even more competitive. Will it be long before law firms in other countries must do so if they are to compete for multi-national business on an even playing field?

BRANDS AND BRANDING

Strategy: Can Martha Stewart be ATTAP?

Marketing wisdom says, "Beware of trying to be ATTAP." (ATTAP stands for All Things To All People.) While this is a potentially dominant marketing strategy, it is also a dangerous one. Brands seldom appeal to everyone. Product categories seldom cross all the customer and market boundaries with equal success. GM messed up its marketing strategy by trying to let each car division have something for everybody. In the end, no division has a clear-cut image for anyone.

After her recent legal troubles and prison stay, Martha Stewart is in more danger than ever of the same type of overreaching. Martha Stewart is a writer of books and cookbooks. Martha Stewart is a daytime TV personality - on a couple of shows. Martha Stewart is a brand name for a wide variety of products for home use, sold by US retailer Kmart. Overexposure is dangerous. When the message is consistent - and Martha Stewart's message has been fairly consistent: "She helps make your home and home life a nicer one" – then it works well. The problem is that such "branded personalities" only realize they have overstepped their bounds after a failure.

Because Martha Stewart herself has this unbounded confidence and energy, that is a real risk. The first clue is a fall off in her TV ratings and advertising demand. When the brand is applied to products that will not carry the premium added to the cost for the "license," that will be the second tip off. Finally, Kmart's corporate performance is a concern. If it has any more financial troubles, it could damage Martha Stewart's name and sales more than anything else could.

It is always dangerous to try being ATTAP. A struggling Kmart and Martha Stewart both need to be careful that this isn't what they are doing with her brand.

REVOLUTION?

Brands: The Boss is back for more people than ever

Hugo Boss clothing once was the province of the high and mighty. In a fashion industry where it is anathema to move downscale, Hugo Boss is trying a revolutionary move. Moving downscale but keeping the upscale cachet is a risky and often impossible move. The Boss brand's success in the 1980s turned into a failure in the 1990s as its exaggerated-shoulder suits and "Where did I put my Lamborghini?" attitude turned off buyers in droves.

Now "the Boss is back" – but at the mall! Hugo Boss is attempting to broaden its base of customers and its distribution by opening stores in US malls. It even signed on as a NASCAR sponsor – a decidedly un-Boss-like move. Boss is pouring champagne near food courts, and catering to middle-American tastes. This is a very risky move, and one that will be difficult to reverse if it doesn't work.

Just in case, Hugo Boss is maintaining a bit of its elitist flavor by hosting splashy premières for movies like *Charlie's Angels* in which actresses Cameron Diaz and Drew Barrymore came decked out in new Boss Woman creations. It is also crossing over to a new audience of status conscious youth by sponsoring a hip-hop tour featuring rappers Eminem and Dr Dre.[4]

So far, sales are up, as are profits. If the trend continues, this will be a risky revolution that succeeded. Have no doubt about it; making a major shift in brand image is a *big* risk . . . unless it works!

INTERNET MARKETING

Brands and branding: What works, what doesn't and why

The Internet spawned a raft of new brand names only to have the companies behind them run out of cash, wither and die. For many it's hard to imagine a life without AOL, eBay, Yahoo! and amazon.com, yet these brands were barely known just a decade ago. Why have they survived when so many others – eToys, Boo.com, Pets.com and their ilk – did not?

First is cash flow. Smart marketing people have learned about cash flow. In a business, cash is like oxygen, profit like food. You can go without food for a while and still live. You can't go without oxygen. The survivors either had marketing and business models that generated positive cash flow, or at least conserved the cash influx from financing. The losers "shot their wads (of cash)" and were gone.

Part of the longevity of the winners is that their brands have become associated with services that are valued, which makes the brands themselves valuable. Another part of it is that these companies (and brands) are the survivors of the shakeouts. AOL won out over CompuServe and Prodigy, among others. Yahoo! outlasted Go, and out-muscled Excite. Amazon.com eclipsed traditional booksellers Barnes & Noble and Borders in on-line selling, and is now a Borders web partner.

As Internet companies consolidated, surviving sites like Yahoo! have done even better. The supply of familiar frequently visited places to advertise is dropping while media is fragmenting more than ever, and that makes Yahoo! a more attractive site for ads. eBay is a natural for the web. It is an interactive form of the garage sale and classified ad in which negotiations and bidding can be done on-line. Its model is perhaps the most economically sound of the web businesses and its marketing has expanded on that model.

Businesses are built on creating and delivering value to customers. Marketing's job is to help interpret what customers would value and then translate that information into action. Ultimately, marketing must communicate the existence of that value so customers know it exists and where to find it. Internet marketing makes some of these tasks easier and some much harder. It is easy to aggregate markets on the web. It is hard to know if broadcast messages and banner ads are really reaching anyone effectively. These issues make the economic analysis of Internet marketing a tough job.

When this works right, the power is enormous. When it doesn't, the disasters are imminent. Branding authority David Aaker puts it this way:

> "... competing in the new economy comes back to some old-time fundamentals. You need to create a loyal customer base by developing favorable brand attitudes. Your offering needs to have vitality and energy that secures your existing base and creates a buzz that interests new customers. It's too bad that so many firms had to run astray of these fundamentals to illustrate the consequences."

Oh yes, there is one more thing. Internet marketing is not alchemy. You need to make a profit - someday - and until you do, you'd better keep the cash flow coming in faster than it goes out!

TRADITIONAL MARKETING

Advertising: Nissan commercials improve business

Nissan was an under-performing Japanese auto company for the past few decades. It trailed leaders Toyota and Honda in profitability and market image. Many critics blamed Nissan's offbeat advertising for the problem, since its cars and trucks were admittedly good products. After creating a series of often baffling and inscrutable commercials Nissan has hit on a winner. The prior commercials may have made sense in Japan, but they left the rest of the world scratching their heads in confusion.

Nissan took a simple approach. It has tapped its leading designer, Jerry Hirshberg, to simply tell people about the products, and back him up with compelling product "hero shots" and added graphics of amazing facts to back up his comments. While prior commercials may have won an occasional creative award, these won the car buyers' votes. Although Hirschberg no longer works for Nissan, he was a major contributor to the company's turnaround. CEO Carlos Ghosn finished the turnaround by creating a company and a series of vehicles that lived up to and extended the commercials hype.

The conclusion to be drawn from this story is that the commercial is not the product. Creative types often become so enamored with the "work of art" that they forget its intended purpose - to communicate in a compelling way with prospective buyers why this product should be the one they choose. When commercials win awards and products don't win sales, you know there is something wrong. Take a minute and reflect on what Nissan learned. Sometimes all the commercial needs to do is to tell the audience why the product is a good one for them to buy. Sound revolutionary? No, but maybe, in a way it is after all.

TRADITIONAL MARKETING

Advertising: Benetton stops gross-out advertising

The huge Italian retailer, Benetton Group, may finally have realized what many discovered before them. Gross-out ads may be memorable, but they don't create sales growth or a positive corporate image. Benetton Group SpA has lost half of its US sales, and now enjoys only 11% of its $1.8bn in revenue in the richest country in the world. Benetton's US store count is down from 600 (in 1987) to only 150.

Much of this decline is attributable to a tasteless advertising campaign that got attention, but the wrong kind of attention. Benetton's ads started positively in the mid 1980s with its United Colors of Benetton, featuring models of different countries and races wearing Benetton clothes. This was perceived to promote racial harmony and world peace – both worthy motives.

Then the campaigns grew more pointed and controversial, as social statements. Ads showing AIDS patients moments before death were followed by ads featuring death row inmates. Few could relate these macabre scenes to a reason to buy Benetton clothing. Boycotts arose in some locales and large conservative customers like Sears dumped the product line. While Benetton still does well in its European base, it has alienated other markets. New ads are being panned in Britain as bland and uninteresting.

Thus the downside of "shock advertising" cuts both ways. It turns off the majority and, when it stops, the extreme minority is vocal about that too. The moral of this story is, don't put gross content in your ads unless you are willing to suffer the equally grim consequences. Gross-out just doesn't sell beyond a small, extremist fringe audience – never has, and hopefully, never will – at least on any large scale.[5]

BRANDS AND BRANDING

Repositioning: Diamonds may be forever, but even monopolies have to be reasonable

DeBeers has ruled the diamond industry for a century by virtue of its lock on the supply from its 13 South African mines. Its vaults hold up to $5bn in uncut diamonds, and its cartel of the largest merchants allow it to manage supply and price in the face of varying world demand.

In recent decades, it has become a marketing company as well, advertising diamonds in a unique and high-class manner. Meanwhile the process by which DeBeers' diamonds come to market is both archaic and effective - at least for controlling the market in a near monopoly fashion. Only the Soviet Union (now defunct) and, to a lesser extent, Australia have diamond deposits large enough to threaten DeBeers' supremacy.

The emergence of valid "competitors" has caused DeBeers to take a different approach to the marketplace. Close scrutiny by US antitrust regulators has also motivated DeBeers to lighten the heavy hand with which it has ruled the diamond market. It is now even talking like a marketer instead of a monopolist. DeBeers' "Supplier of Choice" program is a strategy designed for this new environment.

Supplier of Choice is actually a kind of branding program, incorporating sub-brand elements like its Forevermark, guaranteeing the integrity of DeBeers' diamonds. Using the Forevermark on its famous "diamonds are forever" campaign frees the well-known DeBeers name for other uses. By forming a partnership with French conglomerate LVMH, a retail strategy for using the DeBeers brand can be developed. Additional retailing connections with prestige houses like Escada spread the marketing efforts more broadly.

While DeBeers still controls the majority of the world diamond supply, it now recognizes the role marketing must play in its future. It maintains a $5mn annual marketing department to track buying habits and market potential, including the number of engagements worldwide. Chairman Nicky Oppenheimer says it quite succinctly,

"We want people to say, 'While I can get diamonds from people other than DeBeers, the package DeBeers gives me is so valuable, I get a better return from them'." Even monopolists learn of the need to be marketers eventually.

BRANDS AND BRANDING

Repositioning: Finding sizzle . . . in a padlock?

Marketing is a field in which "much can be made of little" and what better case to use to illustrate that point than the innocuous padlock? For decades, Master Lock was the largest and best-known padlock maker in the US, and its sole advertising theme was that it was "bullet-proof." Its commercial showed the lock being penetrated by a gunshot, but still holding on. This positioning served Master Lock well for a couple of decades, until imported knock offs entered the market undercutting Master Lock's pricing with "looks like" and "works like" copies.

Realizing the threat this presented, Master Lock hooked up with Design Continuum, a West Newton, MA (US) design company. After considerable debate, Master Lock was persuaded to move from a focus on "security and low cost" (a competitive position that played to the import's strength) to one of "it's what's being secured that counts - the lock itself is not that important." While such a move could be dangerous, it let the designers and Master Lock open up a whole new world of possibilities. Why leave padlocks only in the hardware department? How about making colored ones to help kids find their lockers easier? Why not big, friendly buttons and dials on combination locks so the elderly or people wearing gloves (like hunters, contractors, etc.) could easily use them?

What started as a quest for a more attractive padlock became a brand identity revolution. Must Master Locks still be bullet-proof? Sure. Can they look better and be easier to use? Absolutely. The key to marketing is fulfilling the needs of the customer, even when the customer may not realize those needs exist - or can be fulfilled. No one knew they needed FedEx when they didn't know it was possible to get a package anywhere overnight. No one knew padlocks could look totally different, be easier to use, and still be bullet-proof. Now they will!

GLOBALIZATION

Global strategy: Pepsi threatens Coke's supremacy – without the lead in colas

Coke is the "real thing" and everybody around the world knows it - everybody but the new senior management of PepsiCo. New PepsiCo CEO Steve Reinemund finds himself within a short distance of dethroning long time rival Coke without having to do it in a bloody battle over Colas. How? By an end run using "the other drinks"... and snacks that consumers all over the world love to consume.

PepsiCo's profit mix is dominated by the proceeds from its leading $11bn Frito-Lay snack division. Add to that the dominant Tropicana juice brands, a head start in the bottled water business (Aquafina) and the newly acquired Quaker products and PepsiCo is knocking on Coke's door for the title of the world's leading drink company.

Coke can claim victory by definition, carving out the cola market as its domain, but Pepsi may, in fact, become the world's dominant seller of drinks of all kinds. That would make Coke's victory a hollow one indeed - unless that is what Coke wants as its position. Coke, be careful what you wish for - your wish may come true!

GLOBALIZATION

Global strategy: Cadbury Schweppes finds more fun abroad

There is an old saying, "Familiarity breeds contempt," that is often all too true. Perhaps this is part of the problem faced by the premier

British candy maker. The market for its confectionery products, which make up half its volume, is flat or declining slightly in the UK. Competition from global giant Nestlé SA and US-based Mars Inc. is intense.

The good news for Cadbury is that the world is a big place, and its home market, the UK, is just a small part of the big place. Cadbury is opening factories in Russia, China and Poland. These are not easy places to penetrate, but they are large potential markets for a well-known quality candy brand. Cadbury's market position in India (a former British colony) is stronger than that of both Mars and Nestlé, but it is still a small contributor to overall sales and earnings.

Not giving up on its home market, Cadbury is rolling out cafés reminiscent of Starbucks, not so much to make a profit as to promote its brand, do test marketing and evaluate its options. Growing in mature markets against entrenched competitors is a tough road to follow. Going into new, underdeveloped markets is risky, but provides the potential payoff for the risks.

One thing is certain - Cadbury will find more opportunities abroad than in its mature home market - as long as it can figure out how to exploit them profitably. That's where marketing plays a pivotal role.

COLLABORATION

CPFR – A promising new tool

One of the hottest new management tools is an approach called Collaborative Planning Forecasting and Replenishment, or CPFR for short. What is it? CPFR is a cross-industry initiative designed to improve supplier–customer relationships through co-managing the planning and sharing of responsibility for the forecasting and replenishment of goods - primarily for retailers. This new tool goes hand in glove with a marketing initiative called category management.

The CPFR process, developed by a group called the Voluntary Inter-industry Commerce Standards (VICS) Association, defines the best practices and protocols to improve the flow of goods and in stock position (and hopefully sales!) for the partners who use it. This initiative began a few years ago with consultancy Benchmark Partners (now named Surgency), large suppliers like Warner-Lambert and large customers like Wal*Mart seeking better ways to stay in stock, reduce inventory, and improve communications. Supply chain software companies like i2 and Manugistics and ERP software firms like SAP also jumped into the CPFR development process.

A pilot project involved Warner-Lambert's Listerine® mouthwash sold via Wal*Mart stores. The process was first used in a paper-based form and then demonstrated on a computer. In-stock positions for Listerine® rose from 87% to 98%, lead times dropped from 21 to 11 days, and sales increased $8.5mn over the test period even though the test was limited to one Warner-Lambert plant and only three Wal*Mart distribution centers. This was clearly a powerful partnership tool.

The purpose of CPFR is to reduce or eliminate uncertainty through improved communications between supply chain trading partners. This works closely with the goals of the category managers that are trying to maximize the productivity and profit of retail shelf space. The key word in the name is "collaborative."

> Collaborate is defined by Merriam Webster's Collegiate Dictionary as: 1. To work together, especially in a joint effort, and 2. To *cooperate treasonably* as with an enemy occupation force in one's country. What a strange way to describe collaboration – "to cooperate treasonably." This is not as surprising as it might seem, because true collaboration (as in the first definition) is rare enough within companies, and rarer still between companies!

The keys to making CPFR work are similar to those required for category management to work – they require changes in behavior of the people in the partnership - a real challenge. The difficulty is getting all of those using the process to consistently act in the spirit of the collaborative process. Trust is the issue in most collaborative partnerships and this one is no exception. If both partners in the CPFR process realize that the end consumer is their customer, and behave accordingly, the process can work wonders. When they don't, it makes only minor improvements.

Wal*Mart's RetailLink system allows its suppliers to have unparalleled visibility of the performance and status of the goods in Wal*Mart's stores and distribution system. This kind of open information sharing is a hallmark of partnership, and a new marketing tool of epic proportions. Originally known as Manco, the Cleveland, OH (US) division of Henkel KGAA also is a highly collaborative and open company, and its information exchanges with Wal*Mart are a key element of what has become an exemplary partnership. Although they haven't publicly called it CPFR, the relationship has been one of the more productive ones using this methodology. Why? Because the people act, feel and work like partners. Manco category captains support Wal*Mart buyers to make this collaborative process work - and it does. That is the only way any of these new initiatives will realize the greatest benefits for the partners involved.

NOTES

1 "CRM and the Internet - Leading Edge Strategies for a Multi-Channel World." *Business Week*, April 30, 2001.
2 *Ibid*.
3 *Wall Street Journal*, May 15, 2001.
4 Goldman, L., "The Boss is Back." *Forbes*, January 22, 2001.
5 Gallagher, L., "About Face." *Forbes*, March 19, 2001.

In Practice

A number of case studies of organizations are included in this chapter. The cases illustrate different aspects of marketing strategy and/or tactics in use by a wide variety of successful businesses.

PICKING THE RIGHT MARKET SEGMENT

Wyndham Hotels' goal: "not the biggest, but the best"

Knowing what your customer values is key

Wyndham Hotels started in Dallas, TX (US) as part of the ventures of real estate developer Trammel Crow. The name Wyndham was chosen because its meaning in Gaelic is "a winding road to a peaceful place." After merging Wyndham with a larger, but struggling hotel REIT (Real Estate Investment Trust), more than tripling its size, the resulting hotel chain has now emerged as a force in the hotel market.

How can Wyndham do this, at a fraction of the size of hotel giants Hyatt, Hilton, Starwood and Marriott? Simple – stick to your segment and do it superbly. Wyndham has targeted the mid-to-upper class resort and business hotel segment and, with the exception of a couple of properties, mid-size hotels (that's hundreds of rooms, not thousands).

Further, Wyndham has concentrated on the lucrative and highly desirable Caribbean resort market as a cornerstone of its strategy. Hotels in the Caribbean enjoy the temperate weather and are still within the same time zone as the Eastern US, a huge population base. Air service to major Caribbean sites like San Juan and Puerto Rico is excellent, the scenery is wonderful and the beaches inviting.

By targeting the mid-sized business meeting sector (for example, the pharmaceutical industry hosts numerous meetings for doctors to pitch its new drugs), Wyndham can catch lucrative business that spawns return stays for personal vacations. Wyndham has also targeted the traveling businesswoman. As an increasing number of women travel on business, hotels catering to their specific needs and preferences win the close calls in competing for meetings. Another key point is that the majority of corporate meeting planners are females.

Creating the Wyndham "By Request" program, it has developed a repository of traveler preferences in order to "cater to the customer." This membership program is growing rapidly thanks to mass signups by participants in those same corporate meetings. Not only does this allow Wyndham to "know what you like," but it creates a wonderful marketing database for targeted marketing to people who have enjoyed a Wyndham hotel before. The mantra "It's all about you" sums up Wyndham's personalized strategy.

WYNDHAM'S STRATEGY

Since our restructuring in 1999, we have closely aligned our three key products to give us synergies and economies of scale – they use the same central reservations, purchasing and revenue management systems. And we're continuing to improve our existing hotels and add new properties that fit our growth strategy.

Corporate Foundation: We are pursuing our goal of becoming one of the world's premier branded hotel-operating companies from a position of strength. This strength is the result of a solid corporate foundation built on four cornerstones: quality brands and assets, experienced leadership, financial flexibility, and core company values.

Core Values: Wyndham International adheres to six core values, principles that define what the company stands for and encourage a culture of empowerment and excellence. Our values are reflected in how our employees interact with each other and with our guests.

- *Value our People*: Employees are encouraged to help grow and develop themselves and others and to celebrate successes.
- *Value our Customers*: Employees are asked to exceed expectations by taking the initiative to prevent and solve problems and by anticipating and responding to the needs of our guests.
- *Value Respect*: Employees are encouraged to be open-minded and to assume the best of each other. Wyndham embraces the differences in all of us.
- *Value Integrity*: Employees are asked to promise only what they can deliver and to do the right thing in all situations. Wyndham aims to be honest and straightforward in everything we do.
- *Value Accountability*: Employees take ownership of their actions and words. They are encouraged to lead by example and to seek out opportunities to generate win-win solutions.

» *Value Communication*: Employees avoid the confusion that diluted messages can cause by speaking simply and directly. They actively listen and share ideas.

Mission: At Wyndham, we will succeed. Our underlying mission for our guests is constant: to enrich lifestyles through superior hospitality experiences.

http://www.wyndham.com

Wyndham hotels are not all resort destinations. It has several mid-market competitors trying to do something similar, with varying success. Key locations in major cities like Chicago, Boston and Philadelphia are strong complements to its largest city hotel, the 900+ room Anatole Hotel in Dallas, its on-Disney property, the Palace in Orlando, and its most elite hotel, The Boulders, just outside Phoenix, AZ (US). By creating second tier (size) hotels in key city locations it can retain a high-value luxury image just under the umbrella of top end competitors like Ritz-Carlton and Four Seasons.

By targeting mid-size meetings, the hotels can tailor meeting space to the target market needs. Since Wyndham, by virtue of its heritage, owns about 80% of its hotel properties, it also has greater control of what kind of "deals" it can make and support. Most large hotel chains own a far lower percentage of properties, making expansion less costly, but forcing them to compromise with owners on the deals and arrangements made with meeting planners. The larger hotels are also the primary listings for large conventions, but then must turn over a large percentage of rooms to the convention for assignment, a double edged sword – filling capacity, but giving up control of how and who fills it.

Since the "new" Wyndham broke on the scene just a few short years ago, it has also done one of the smartest things any marketer can do. It has attracted top talent from other chains – people who like the concept of "being the best, if not the biggest." This talent, combined with attractive properties in excellent locations, makes Wyndham's marketing strategies good ones to watch and emulate in other industries.

The lessons: define the target market segment and tailor products that serve it very well; *being the best, if not the biggest* is a good theme for anyone who doesn't want to (or can't afford to) take on the entrenched large competitors. Making it *all about you* reinforces the theme of service to customers and personalization in an increasingly depersonalized business world.

TRYING TO GET BIG BY STAYING "SMALL"

Best Buy – A leader grows based on customer focus

Having everything the customer wants, and helping them find it

Best Buy is clobbering the competition in the consumer electronics market. The behemoth from Minnesota is beating competitors like Circuit City and CompUSA with its new-found size and strategy. Best Buy wasn't always big. In fact, in 1966 it started small, with a single store called Sound of Music in St Paul, MN (US). Now that it has grown to nearly 2000 stores and 75,000 employees, it is trying to "get small" all over again.

Obviously, the huge Best Buy stores that offer everything a consumer could imagine in electronics and related products can't physically "get smaller." How Best Buy is doing it is through a combination of people, layout and technology - specifically something called CRM - Customer Relationship Management. Best Buy stores are a visual, audio-sensory experience for the first time shopper. Thousands of products spread over thousands of square feet could be impossibly dazzling and just confuse shoppers. Best Buy reduces confusion from its stores' overwhelming size and assortment through the use of lower fixtures that allow long lines of sight for finding the area you want, signage that points out the major areas, and zoned merchandising.

Once you find the general area you want, logical merchandise arrays and floor sales help take over. The CRM system doesn't kick in until you have bought something and become a prospective customer for related items. Then the computers notice that you bought a digital receiver, but not a DVD player; or a digital camera but not a photo quality printer. You will be likely to get an offer to buy one of those at a special discount. And in many cases you will buy, or at least go look, and that is another opportunity for Best Buy.

> "It is hell to be a consumer today.
> A company needs to work like crazy to make things easy for the customer."
> *Mike Linton, Sr VP for Strategic Marketing, Best Buy*

Once you have bought something, to give you that safe, "We'll take care of you" feeling that smaller stores once had, Best Buy will sell you one of its 3-Year Performance Service Plans. There is nothing so revolutionary about most of these elements. Other retailers sell service plans - among them CompUSA. Mail order retailer Viking Office Products grew and prospered by using customer information on prior purchases to target future promotional offers. What is unique is putting all of these elements together in a "big box" retail setting that makes it the one-stop destination for anything Best Buy carries. That is a powerful marketing advantage.

Add to all this the buying and vendor promotional support Best Buy can earn by its volume and retail presentation, and the competitors all seem a weak second best. Competitors are trying, but not gaining on Best Buy. CompUSA changed its format and assortment to emulate part of Best Buy's, but has less square footage in which to sell, so it is limited. Its name, once an advantage, is now somewhat limiting too - consumers expect it to have "computer stuff." Circuit City is conceding some areas to bolster its efforts in others. Large appliances are gone from Circuit City, but not from Best Buy. While this move may have been the best thing for Circuit City to do, it steered still more consumers to Best Buy's big stores. Regional electronics chains suffer from similar problems as the national ones in competing with Best Buy.

Consumer traffic is precious - and considered purchases like large appliances draw both men and women - and getting women into a consumer electronics store is not so easy. Once there, both genders can be attracted by whatever catches their eye - DVDs or tapes of popular movies, computers and software, home appliances, telephones of all kinds, and so much more. But all of this is not easy.

The ultimate test of this strategy will come in the long term success Best Buy has in consolidating databases and putting that information into use where it will do the most good - on the sales floor and in promotional campaigns. VP of CRM Systems Scott Lien says, "No matter where the customer interacts with the enterprise - across a number of brands or channels - we have a single customer view." The question is whether Best Buy can get its numerous floor sales people "connected" to use the information it has. In retailing, the largest challenges are always centered on people and execution.

Gartner Dataquest's Jeff Roster thinks the retailer is on the right track. He puts it this way, "If I were a retailer, I'd be doing exactly what they're doing." But then he adds, "You can have the best Super Bowl game plan ever, but if your players drop passes and miss blocks you are not going to win."[1]

Best Buy is winning so far on the strength of overwhelming the competition.

- In the future, the key to marketing success is in being able to integrate excellent execution with superb strategy.
- To do this, people are the key element!

THE NEW LOOK OF RETAIL

Sephora - changing the rules of the shopping experience

Making it fun and easy for the consumer is a good idea

French born cosmetics company Sephora has revolutionized the retail shopping experience in cosmetics. When a male (like myself) goes in a cosmetics store and wishes there were something he could shop for there, that store has achieved something tremendous. (Note: US electronics retailer Best Buy is on that threshold, as evidenced by my wife's reaction when I dragged her into one of its stores.)

Sephora, now a part of world fashion leader LVMH, has created retail stores that appeal to the consumer by breaking age-old rules. The store is dramatic - black and white décor and walls of video screens adding to the flair. Staff are dressed accordingly, in black, with one black glove on the hand used to show off jewelry like perfume bottles.

The products provide the color in the store. Massive arrays of products arranged not by manufacturer (old way) but by color (for lipstick) or alphabetically (for perfumes). The assortment is vast and the visual effect is dazzling. Most of all, shopping is fun and merchandise is easy to find in spite of the huge assortments.

In department stores, high-end cosmetics and beauty products generate a huge, disproportionate amount of profits - as much as 20% of the total store profits. Why do you think the stores and manufacturers pay for commissioned salespeople to intercept customers as they walk through with a spritz of perfume, or do a free facial "makeover" on the spot?

Sephora has turned this model on its head too. Staff are salaried, not commissioned. Manufacturers, much to their chagrin, have little control over the displays, or the sales techniques. Just as US discounter Target created a more pleasing discount store shopping appearance by prohibiting suppliers' displays and creating a uniform, clean appearance in the store, so too has Sephora.

Author Gary Hamel cites this example in his book *Leading the Revolution* (Harvard Business School Press, 2000). He describes the strategy this way. "Business concept innovation isn't strictly about *competitive* strategy. It is not a way of positioning *against* competitors, but of going *around* them. It's based on *avoidance*, not *attack*. Here's the key though: *what is not different is not strategic*."

Look at what Sephora has done in marketing and selling strategy to be different:

Marketing & selling strategy	Old way	Sephora way
Commissioned sales staff	Yes	No
Gift with purchase	Yes	No
Each counter with one brand	Yes	No
Displays controlled by manufacturer	Yes	No
Shop alone, minimal sales interference	No	Yes
Samples easily available	No	Yes
Products grouped - easy comparison	No	Yes
Customer in control	No	Yes

Are these just different for difference's sake? I don't think so. They are different to recognize that the customer wants these things - unmolested shopping, easy choice, accessible sampling, etc. Some cosmetics companies have withheld certain product lines from Sephora, but this is a sign that the Sephora model is working. Manufacturers around the world prefer to control marketing and distribution, and revolutionary retailers usually disrupt that control.

US retailers have been doing just this for a decade or more: Wal*Mart, Costco, Target, Toys R Us have all struggled with product restrictions vs traditional upscale retailers like department stores and specialty shops, but the barriers are rapidly crumbling. (The Internet is another shopping system where withholding products doesn't seem to work very well.)

By the spring of 1999 Sephora had captured 20% of the French retail cosmetics market and its march around the world had begun. Within 18 months of opening its first store in New York, Sephora had opened 50 across the US, and had plans for many more. Such stores take large traffic and large sales, and thus will ultimately be self-limiting as to their number. But until they are, cosmetics retailers will feel the squeeze of this powerful new retailing technique.

What is Sephora's success based on?

» It is putting the customer first.
» Making it easy for the customer to find, try, choose or not.
» It is about making shopping an experience, not just a necessity.

Those are powerful marketing lessons.

DESIGN AND TECHNOLOGY IS A COMMANDING ADVANTAGE

Sony – combining the entire electronic experience

Making a better, nicer, more integrated product line at premium prices and profits

Japanese electronics maker Sony has been a world leader in quality consumer electronics for the past few decades. It has elevated its brand into the top five in the world, and its marketing and product strategy is a wonder to behold. For years, Sony was a leader in electronic entertainment, which was then defined as music and video equipment - like TVs and stereo receivers. It literally created the portable tape player market with its Walkman®, followed by the Watchman® and then the Discman® for CDs. Sony's Trinitron TV sets were the "gold standard" of high quality television sets. Naturally this tube technology found its way into comparably high quality computer monitors, but that was only the beginning.

As Sony saw the electronics market morphing into a continuous array of personal and home entertainment for audio, video, and then computer equipment, its design and marketing machinery went into action. Now Sony has a full range of products that are all compatible, and of the highest performance and quality. The VAIO computer line revolutionized the lightweight laptop market a few years ago with a 2.5lb., three-eighths-inch thick, full function laptop computer. Not long after this, a video camera was integrated into the lid of a variation of this laptop to create the "PictureBook." Not only were the products revolutionary, but so were the names (except for "VAIO," which most consumers had trouble pronouncing and even fewer could easily remember what it stood for - including this writer; I just know it's "Video-Audio . . . something").

But Sony did not stop there. It collaborated with world-renowned lens maker Zeiss and introduced a top quality digital camera line, with features like the ability to make short MPEG movies with the same camera used for top quality still photos. There was even a big accessory market created for its small but expensive (and highly profitable) memory cards. The more one does with the camera, the bigger the memory card that is needed - at a cost of over $100 per card for a camera that only cost $300–900.

MP3 exploded onto the scene as Internet music "bandits" like Napster made digital music something accessible to anyone with a computer and a high-speed connection (or a lot of patience). Sony was all over this trend too, maintaining its leadership in portable electronics. As DVDs take over from videotapes in music and movies, Sony won't have another Betamax (wrong format) fiasco. It will be in the thick of the DVD player race as well.

Not to be outpaced by game specialists Nintendo and Sega, Sony rocked the world in 2000 with its game player, Playstation, for which it underestimated demand and put retailers in a situation of having a scarce but hot commodity at Christmas. This mattered little in the long run. Sony had staked out its marketing leadership in yet another electronic entertainment segment.

A more recent Sony product getting kudos from experts is an improvement on the widely accepted Palm family of PDA (Personal Digital Assistant). Although it too is named a bit obliquely as Clié (Clee-ay), its quality and performance is Sony-like. In other words, a notch above the competition at a modest price premium.

The critical lesson here is that the technology across these products is similar, complementary, and buying one can lead to buying another - for assured compatibility if not for better performance and style (i.e., several can share the use of those same expensive little memory cards).

The other lesson is that consistent technical performance, styling and quality leadership allows a marketer to expand across a densely populated, competitive playing field like a battalion of tanks crossing the desert in Desert Storm - laying waste to competitors who stand in the way. Before long, young people may not be singing *"I want my MTV."* They will more likely be singing *"I want my SONY."*

SPEED IS A POWERFUL MARKETING WEAPON

Zara – a captive supply chain combined with design and marketing

Fast turns yield fast info and fast success

I first described Zara in my 2000 book, *Smart Things to Know about Marketing*. Since then, the world has discovered it and publicized it much more broadly. Zara is a Spanish retailer, headquartered in the port city of La Coruña. Zara's parent company, Inditex, has built a $2bn chain of 937 stores in 31 countries. What makes Zara special is the speed with which it turns its merchandise and styles. Zara sends out a few thousand skirts during the night to some of its 449 stores worldwide to test the waters on a new design or style. If the product is a hit, more are in the stores in a matter of weeks. Twice weekly, clothes are delivered to its shops, and consumers react by flocking in to see what's new. Competing with stores like Gap, which built its advantage on rapid logistics, Zara is raising the speed bar another notch. Zara takes four to five weeks to design a new collection and a week to make it. Competing chains take an average of *six months* to design a new collection and then *three more months* to make it and get it moving toward the stores.

Using tight control of design and production, Zara can take a trend from catwalk to sidewalk in as little as two weeks. How does Zara do all this? First, it owns the factories and its own distribution network. In an era when vertical integration is passé, Zara has found a way to integrate its supply chain and creative product design and marketing into a high-speed machine that surpasses competitors like Benetton SpA of Italy, by a huge amount. The faster trends make it into the stores, the faster the readout on how consumers like them - and buy them - or not! This rapid information feedback loop allows replacement of poor sellers with new styles very quickly. Whether this speed can be rolled out across oceans is still to be seen, but in the meanwhile, fast response leads to fast feedback, which leads to even faster response. And one thing that is proven over and over is that, the sooner you know how consumers like something, the better off you are. The other important point is that the best market research is based on customers voting with money.

There are some downsides to the Zara method. First, it takes money to own the supply chain as much as it does. Some complain that Zara's clothing quality leaves something to be desired - but with the rapid fashion change model, clothing need not last a long time. New designs make old ones obsolete. None the less, Zara is determined to improve quality too, and some of its new lines are showing improvement. There is a risk of lost flexibility and reduced input from outside suppliers, but Zara is getting some of that too. It listens to customers "like a sponge," says designer Rafael Pastor. Beatriz Padim, a *comercial*, is part designer, part fashion consultant and, as part of her job, she scans fashion magazines for new looks and speeds them into production for market tests.

The results of these tests are the best kind of market research - where customers vote for the products they like with money - they buy them! "Hits" are rushed into broader distribution, and "misses" are quietly closed out and disposed of.

Store management even assists in creating the rapid "new merchandise" cycle and image by moving goods to different locations in stores. In this way, the consumers get a new look each time they visit the store. The rapid cycles create an urgency to buy - that item and style may be gone soon, so "buy it now!" No one wants to wear the same thing as everyone else - or to miss out on the latest fashion.

Here is a European retailer that is on a roll by integrating design and marketing with its lightning fast supply chain, and basing its decisions on real consumers' purchases instead of theoretical market research studies.

GOING BACK TO YOUR ROOTS IS A GOOD IDEA

Volkswagen-US rebuilds its market position with product excellence

Give customers what they want to buy, not what you want to sell

This is a classic success story of a company that resurrected its product line and brand from the scrap heap in the US market. In 1970, VW sold 570,000 vehicles in the US. Its Beetle, Minibus and Kharmann Ghia sport models were the symbols of the 1960s generation. VW was so successful that it decided to build a US plant - in Pennsylvania - to produce cars closer to the huge and profitable US market.

Then disaster struck. In the process of building the US plant, there was the requisite deliberation about what the plant would make. You don't build a new plant to run old products, the Germans thought. The serious German management could not understand these crazy Americans and how they "made fun of" VW cars. And the Beetle and Minibus were getting a bit long in the tooth. Their rear mounted and air-cooled engines were anachronisms compared to contemporary engine technology. Emerging US pollution, safety and crash resistance standards would have required some additional design revisions. The small flower vase on the dash was a potential hazard in a collision. So, the Germans stopped selling the fun products and introduced a suitably serious product line to the US plant. Bad mistake!

The new cars, the Golf (isn't that a game, not a car?), and the Jetta (what's that anyway?) were greeted with a resounding ho-hum. These cars were excellent works of German engineering with all the excitement and fun value of a brick. VW sales plummeted to a low of 49,500 units in 1993. This was a brand and a company that was almost out of the US market. Dealers failed, merged, and ran for cover. Not only was the VW brand damaged, but also then its upscale Audi line was the primary victim of the accidental acceleration scare. There were dark days in the US arm of Europe's largest auto maker, and it all had to do with marketing missteps and product design errors.

Then, a decade later, someone finally got smart at VW. Nostalgia was big in the US. Baby boomers were yearning for the simpler days of a bygone era. The VW Beetle was a symbol, an icon of that generation. But, sadly, it was only made in Mexico and was suitable for import to the US only after expensive safety and pollution modifications. But really, VW knew how to make good cars, so it started with that skill. VW's creative designers added some whimsy (you want a Beetle - well, here's a new one - just like the old one, including the bud vase on the dash, but better mechanically) for the "crazy Americans" and some sizzling style for the upscale baby boomers, and voilà! - the new Volkswagen and Audi lines.

Led by the rebirth of the Beetle (but with Audi-like mechanicals and platform), VW began its resurgence. The new, redesigned Audi line parlayed tasteful and sophisticated styling and all-wheel-drive into a solid niche position among the big luxury automakers Mercedes-Benz, BMW, and Lexus. Then VW "knocked off" its own Audi styling to make the new Jetta and Passat models to sell alongside the Beetle. When the cars are good enough, obtuse (but now familiar) names are OK.

By 2001, VW sold well over 300,000 cars in the US and this growing level of sales was fueled by its clever "Drivers wanted" advertising campaign emphasizing the combination of visual uniqueness and excellent driveability. Even offbeat new paint colors and a limited edition series reinforced the unique personality of the new Beetle - just like the old one. Buyers went wild. VW was "back" in the US market.

VW is now a solid player in the US market. Why?

- Because it decided to sell what its customers wanted to buy and not what it wanted to sell!
- Marketing products built on VW's technical strength was a great platform, and it made certain that was what its brand delivered - a brand is a promise and a relationship - and VW kept both.

"It ain't what you don't know that'll kill you. It's what you think you know that ain't so!"

Will Rogers

NOTE

1 Moore, M.M., "Thinking Small." *Darwin*, May 2001.

Key Concepts and Thinkers

This chapter defines and explains many of the most commonly used terms in the field.

One of the prerequisites to understanding what a book is talking about is to understand some of the phrases, buzz words and specialized terms that describe marketing in use. The definitions that follow cover the "most common" marketing vocabulary and practices. There is also a list of terms and definitions in the chapter on the e-dimension, since the Internet era has created a lot of its own unique vocabulary.

- *Account management*: The front line contact with customers (accounts) and the assurance that the customer's needs are understood and met. Also that the customer's decision-maker understands all of your products or services that might be desirable to them.
- *Advertising and promotion plans*: The part of the communications plan specifically dealing with planned communications intended to inform/persuade a current or prospective purchaser of the desirability of a product or service.
- *Advertising terms*: CPM, Rating points, SOA, SOV, SOM.
  - *CPM*: Cost Per Thousand is advertising shorthand for what it costs to reach a thousand people in the target market with the advertising. This can vary widely and, in the case of Internet advertising, raises questions of how to measure advertising.
  - *Rating points*: A measure of how well advertising is intended to and actually reaches a given audience. Calculated by multiplying the "Reach" times the "Frequency." Reach is the percentage of the target market the ad is seen or heard by, and Frequency is the number of times those people saw or heard it. The term Target Rating Points (TRP) refers to the rating points in the target market. Gross Rating Points (GRP) refers to the rating points in the total market.
  - *SOA*: Share of Advertising is the actual measured share of advertising expenditures for competing products targeting the same product/service consumers in the same media markets. In simple terms, what share of the ad media spending was yours?
  - *SOV*: Share of Voice is a measure of viewership (or readership) share as a result of an advertising campaign - in other words, how much of the "voice" of all the advertising run against that product/service and market did your advertising constitute?
  - *SOM*: Share of Market is the bottom line - based on actual sales outcomes. In simplest terms, who sold what percentage of a given

category of product/service in a specified market segment over a specified time frame? This is what most advertisers want to achieve, because this is where money is made - other measures are just how much is being spent for how much relative "noise" it makes.

» *Annoyance marketing*: The intrusive, "in-your-face" approach to marketing, in which the prospect is accosted with unwanted messages regardless of their desire for those messages. Examples - telemarketing, banner ads and pop up windows, handbills, excessively loud or tasteless radio or TV ads, etc.
» *Blitz*: An attack on a given segment of a market with excessive resources, product offerings, distribution, promotion, etc. (Any number of dot-com companies - like monster.com - spent advertising money freely competing for position in an overcrowded market.)
» *Brand management*: Brand or category managers are entrusted with assets that are far more valuable than the company's buildings and equipment. They must ensure that the brands, products, and programs are developed, supported and portrayed in a manner consistent with the image they represent in the minds of consumers. The management of all the activities and resources to do this is the job of the brand manager.
» *Budgets*: The projections of what revenue will be earned or funds will be spent, classified by accounts describing the source of revenues and the nature of expenses. Usually made for calendar periods - months, quarters and years, and classified by functional departments, divisions, product lines or other relevant breakdowns.
» *Capital expenditures*: Larger expenditures having longer term impact on the business usually to acquire a fixed asset or meet other major needs of the business, such as facilities, machinery, equipment, information systems, software, etc.
» *Category captains*: A term to describe the supplier personnel who assist and support retail customers in the management of the planning and merchandising of the categories in which their products are offered.
» *Category management*: The management of the merchandising, supply, pricing, display, presentation and promotion of an entire category of products. Most commonly used in retail settings.

- *Collateral materials and support*: The information made up of catalogs, product specification sheets, flyers, handouts, displays, etc. which enhance the sale of the product either by aiding the sales force or informing the customer or consumer.
- *Communications plan*: The comprehensive listing of events, time frames and budgets for telling current and prospective purchasers, and many others (including suppliers, employees, and investors) about the entire product/service offerings of a company and how these are superior to competition or beneficial to customers.
- *Competitive analysis*: A detailed, quantitative breakdown of the strengths and weaknesses, advantages and disadvantages of competitors and communicating their relative position to customers, clients and prospects.
- *Conjoint analysis*: Conjoint analysis is the name given to the application of an analytical technique called "design of experiments" to obtaining insights into individual customer preferences. An important result is that the output is the quantified preference of an individual for a set of attributes of a product/service, etc. This set of individual preferences can then be used with others to simulate an entire market.
- *Consumer*: The end-user who finally puts the product or service to its intended use.
- *Cost of Goods Sold (COGS)*: The total of the Material + Labor + Overhead in a traditional system, or Material + Fixed and Variable Conversion Cost in an Activity Based Cost system.
- *Customer Relationship Management (CRM)*: CRM is a new "buzzword" for age-old processes translated to the new, computer/web based economy. Its devotees describe CRM as "the overall process of marketing, sales, and service within any organization." CRM (and PRM) systems (are supposed to) help businesses develop and sustain profitable customer and partner relationships - and maybe they do. Companies are investing in CRM in hopes of gaining competitive differentiation in a world where products become commodities overnight. *But there is no replacement for good old-fashioned customer relationships - between people - not computers!*
  - *PRM or Partner Relationship Management*: A subset of CRM - "the application of Relationship Management strategies and technologies to the unique needs of indirect sales channels."

- » *Campaign management*: The use of customer information from databases or transaction records to plan, target and manage promotional campaigns.
- » *Personalization*: The use of information and/or web technology to analyze buying habits of customers and predict which products or services those customers are likely to buy next and when - and then offer those by direct mail or web access.
- » *Customer-centricity*: Building business strategies based on what customers are most inclined to buy rather than on what the supplier company is most inclined to sell.
- » *Lifetime value*: A calculation of how much business a given customer is likely to do with a given supplier over its lifetime less the cost to acquire and keep that customer.

» *Customer service (after the sale)*: A function which assures that questions, problems and issues arising after a sale is made are satisfactorily answered or resolved for the customer or the consumer.

» *Customer*: The person and/or company who chooses, buys and pays for the product or service.

» *Distribution*: The process of identifying, aggregating and transporting products from their point of production or storage to the location where the customer can make them available to consumers or end users for purchase and use.

» *EBIT*: Earnings Before Interest and Taxes.

» *EBITDA*: Earnings Before Interest, Taxes, Depreciation and Amortization.

» *Economic analysis*: A financial analysis that determines how a planned course of action will result in economic outcomes and the relative desirability of those outcomes versus goals and objectives.

» *End run*: Instead of a frontal assault on the market position of an entrenched competitor, altering some of the specifications, features, services or programs and going after an exposed flank. Perhaps attacking a weaker product, a vulnerable customer position, or remote piece of geography and then working in to the larger pieces of the business.

» *Expenses*: The expenditures made on a day-to-day basis in the normal course of doing business to support and enable the business to operate.

- *Feasibility*: Whether something can be done - e.g., whether a given product can be developed which will perform certain functions and meet specifications within a given cost and price level.
- *Features and specifications*: The definition of what the product or service will do and how it achieves that end, usually in some measurable quantitative terms that are meaningful to a large community of constituents including customers, suppliers, distributors, etc.
- *Feedback*: The flow of information back to the originator of the topic.
- *Gross profit*: the selling price minus the cost of goods sold.
- *Gross profit margin*: The value remaining after subtracting the Cost of Goods Sold (plus or minus any variances) from the Net Selling Price. (If it is to be expressed as a percentage, it is calculated by dividing the gross profit by the selling price.)
- *Guerilla attack*: To go after an important pieces of business either with a clandestine and/or varied attack (in location, strategy, pricing, etc.) in hopes of undermining a much larger competitor in a particular market niche. (Apple Computer rebuilding market share vs. Dell, Compaq, HP, IBM, *et al.*)
- *Hits*: Sometimes called "clicks" or "visits," the term for the number of times a web page or part of a page is visited.
- *Implementation steps*: Often called by other names (see below), these are the discrete statements that describe "how" the strategies will be pursued and achieved.
- *Intellectual property*: Proprietary concepts or ideas embodied in products or services, which may be granted protection in legal forms of trade marks, patents, copyrights, or protected by trade secret laws, etc.
- *Launch plans*: Detailed specific plans for strategies, implementation steps, tactics, actions, results, timetables, budgets, resources and accountabilities for the introduction of a product or service to a market.
- *Logistics*: The deployment of people and materials to assure that a given mission is completed according to plan. With respect to marketing, the process of assuring that the right thing will be in the right place, in the right quantity, at the right time and the right cost.

» *Margin (or profit margin or gross margin)*: The amount of difference between what a given product costs to acquire in terms of material, labor, overhead, etc. and what it will sell for. Usually calculated as a gross margin by dividing the gross profit by the selling price and expressing that as a percentage.
» *Market attack*: To aggressively go after a major position in a given market by deploying substantial resources with a product or service offering that is at parity (or better) with entrenched competition. Usually used by large industry leaders (e.g. AT&T, when they launched their digital wireless phone service).
» *Market definition*: The way one defines the segment (group) of customers to be pursued. Usually segments are defined in terms of geography, lifestyle, product/service needs, age/demographics, psychographics, economics, and many other factors.
» *Market opportunity analysis*: A specific, orderly method by which the potential of a given market is analyzed for the opportunity it presents to prospective suppliers in terms of the needs and desires of current or potential customers. What is the opportunity - in the markets you have chosen to target or, conversely, for the products you have chosen to sell?

"Value is as your customers perceive it, and so every organization must find ways to draw out from customers how they see value - now and in the future. For this reason, 'identify the value' is where planning a customer value delivery strategy must begin . . . by the time you begin a customer value determination process, you must already know which current or potential customers are strategically important . . . Identifying these customers is one activity in a market opportunity analysis . . ."

Woodruff, R. and S. Gardial (1996) Know Your Customer. Blackwell, Oxford

» *Market opportunity hierarchy*: That is the concept of customer value hierarchies. We all think in terms of attributes of products. The car has air bags and anti-lock brakes, which describe the product and the "hardware."

  - Attributes are at the bottom level of the hierarchy. We really choose those attributes because we want to enjoy the consequences of them – personal safety in a collision and better control/stopping under adverse driving conditions.
  - Consequences are the mid-level of the hierarchy. Ultimately, we chose those attributes because we recognized the consequences would lead to meeting higher order needs or desired end-states – a safer, more secure environment for ourselves and our loved ones who ride with us.
  - Higher order needs or desired end-states located at the top of the hierarchy are what we are really willing to pay for, and these are a much more stable target to aim for.
  - Understanding this hierarchy is important – using it to guide marketing decisions is smart!
- *Market research*: A term which encompasses a large number of tools, techniques and methods used to learn more about markets, customers, products/services, and other aspects of creating, marketing and selling products and services.
- *Market research (types)*: Surveys; focus groups; intercepts; questionnaires; in-depth interviews; internet research; and many more.
- *Markup*: Another term for expressing the profit on a sale as a percentage but calculated by dividing the profit by the cost.
- *Measures*: The quantitative metrics by which success against plans, goals and objectives are to be measured.
- *Milestones*: Checkpoints at which progress is to be measured. Can be based on actions, time, economic results, and many other criteria.
- *Mix*: The specific mixture of an assortment of products and product groups which make up an overall product line sold or being offered for sale – usually defined by the percentage that each item and sub-group is of the total group, product line or business.
- *Order fulfillment*: The process of receiving the communicated needs of the customer and re-communicating those needs in such a way that the specific products or services to meet those needs are provided/delivered to the customer.
- *Packaging*: the materials which contain, protect, identify and present/enhance a product during its movement from the producer to the customer and ultimately to the end user.

» *Permission marketing*: A new relatively term (coined by Seth Godin in the book of the same name), to describe marketing in a more customer friendly relationship and less intrusive manner. One in which the customer is actually given a choice to grant or withhold permission to be a target of a marketing campaign. (For more, see The E-Dimension.)
» *Positioning*: The place a product occupies in the mind of customers, consumers and prospects. Al Ries and Jack Trout made this term popular two decades ago in their book *Positioning - The Battle for Your Mind*.

> "Positioning starts with a product . . . *But positioning is not what you do to a product*. Positioning is what you do with the mind of the prospect. That is, you position the product in the mind of the prospect. Anyone can use positioning strategy to get ahead in the game of life. And look at it this way. If you don't understand and use the principles, your competitors undoubtedly will." (My emphasis added.)
> *Al Ries and Jack Trout, Positioning - The Battle for your Mind*

» *Price signaling*: To make price adjustments in such a prominent and obvious way as to encourage other participants in the market to follow those moves. Used by industry leaders or members of an oligopoly (e.g., major airlines' ticket prices).
» *Product life cycle*: A series of stages which all products move through:
  » Stage 1 - Market development: When a new product is first brought to market with proven demand but before it has been fully developed. Growth is slow; sales are low.
  » Stage 2 - Market growth: Demand begins to accelerate and market size expands rapidly - also called the "takeoff stage."
  » Stage 3 - Market maturity: Demand levels off and grows only at replacement or intrinsic market growth rates.
  » Stage 4 - Market decline: Loss of consumer appeal, sales drift downward more and more.
» *Product line matrix*: An array with products listed down one side and relative prices, costs, margins, and other characteristics listed

across the top, showing the relevant data at the intersections. Usually done using a spreadsheet program.

- *Product line structure*: The relationship between various products and family groupings of products relative to other offerings, usually with regard to prices and features/specifications.
- *Product line/business portfolios*: A method of categorizing products or businesses into logical groupings based on characteristics such as growth rate, profitability, market size, share, etc.
- *Product planning*: The process of designing the product lines and specific products to match a strategy for a given target market segment including time frames, resources, product line structure, etc.
- *Product/service acquisition*: Often called sourcing, procurement, purchasing, production, operations, etc. This consists of actually getting/making the product or service to be sold.
- *Product/service*: The value provided in exchange for the sacrifice made (usually in currency, but also in time, effort, etc.) to obtain the "thing" which is deemed desirable and valuable.
- *Production*: The process of converting purchased raw materials and components into salable finished products.
- *Project management*: Project management is the management, allocation and control of resources - people, money and time - to complete some specific set of goals and objectives within a defined time schedule.
- *Public relations*: The process of communicating newsworthy information to the general public, usually via mass media, but which supports or promotes a product, a brand, or a broader marketing objective.
- *Retaliation*: To attack a competitor in a lucrative market segment as a direct result of that competitor attacking one of your important segments. Can be used by any type or size of company, with varying success (e.g., Microsoft going after Sun's Java programs).
- *Return on investment*: The economic return earned as a direct result of a particular investment, usually calculated in an equivalent annual percentage rate compared to the total investment.
- *Sales strategies*: Approaches by which the customer will be persuaded to choose a given offering over the competing ones.

- *Sales support and presentation*: The materials, methods, processes and people behind the scenes who prepare and sometimes help deliver sales messages to customers. May also include those who provide follow-up support such as sending out samples, promised detail information, etc. after a sales call or presentation.
- *Secure servers*: The servers which handle financial information and process transactions like stock trades, credit card transactions, etc. on the Internet, and provide information security at a much higher level than openly sending confidential information over the Internet.
- *Situation analysis*: The definition of the environment and conditions in a particular competitive or market segment at a given point in time.
- *Sourcing*: Selection and negotiation of terms of business with the source (supplier) for a given product or service.
- *Sponsorships and spokespersons*: Promotional devices in which well-known and/or respected people endorse or speak on behalf of products or services and add desirability to the items they endorse.
- *Strategies*: Statements that describe "what" is planned to be done to achieve a particular set of goals and objectives, usually at the business unit level, but applicable at any level.
- *Tactics or operational action plans*: A more detailed level of specific behaviors, tasks and actions intended to support the implementation steps and strategies and lead to achieving specific near-term goals and objectives.
- *Target market examples*: Every marketing plan has (or should have) a target market. The target market is the audience you have identified that you want the ads for your product or service to reach. It is the market to which you want to sell your brand, value proposition and goods/services. These target markets are often described in different ways. Here is a partial listing of some ways to segment target markets:
  - *Age demographics*, such as "ages 13–25" or other age categories broken down into market segments or to match census data used for analysis.
  - *Gender* – male or female.
  - *Minorities* (using the US as an example) African-American, Hispanic, Asian, etc.

  - *Job, career or profession* - working mothers, two-income families, white-collar or blue-collar, etc.
  - *Geo-political areas* - cities, states, provinces, counties, or others within defined boundaries (a common term used in advertising is SMSA - Standard Metropolitan Statistical Area - the area surrounding a major city and measured/influenced by its media/advertising coverage).
  - *Life-stage* - deals with the age and interest level of the consumer based on the stage of life they are in.
  - *Activity* - a key form of segmentation based on the activity preferences of the group. Many other segments that might be of interest can be defined by combining market segments in specific ways, such as parents of children in specific age groups, households with certain income levels, special interest groups, retirees, etc.
- *Target segment*: The specific part of the market in terms of some measurable or definable characteristic.
- *Tie-in and cross-branded/co-branded promotions*: Any of a wide variety of marketing efforts where multiple brands collaborate to share the exposure and reach mutual goals. Examples: Oreo® Cookies mixed in branded ice creams; M & Ms® or Snickers® used with TCBY® Yogurt; Coach® leather goods and Lexus® autos, Eddie Bauer® and Ford® SUVs, etc.
- *Unique visitors*: The description of unique computers which "hit" a Website, even though they may click on many pages or items within the site. Loosely analogous to "customer visits in a retail store" even though there may be no purchase made.
- *Viability*: Whether a product or service which can meet the test of "feasibility" can be sold in sufficient volumes for a sustained period of time to earn an acceptable return on the investment required for its creation, production and distribution.
- *Working capital*: The money required to pay for facilities, goods and services necessary to produce, acquire and deliver products until the purchasers have paid for them.

09

Resources

This chapter provides an excellent overview of references that the reader can use to build a broader understanding of the field.

*These are the top ten high priority resources . . . check them out first.

*Aaker, David A., in *Strategy and Business*, 2Q (2000). Aaker has done more research and written more on brands than almost anyone lately. He is an important author for brand builders. Both of his books on the topic - *Managing Brand Equity* and *Building Strong Brands*, The Free Press, New York - are excellent.

*Blackwell, Roger D. (with Stephan, Kristina). His new book, *Customers Rule*, is a timely look at the power of marketing amid the stumbles of e-commerce. In the article, "The Retail Paradigm," *Retail Merchandiser*, July (2000) (Blackwell, Roger D. and Stephan, Kristina), Roger Blackwell's wisdom is applied to retailing.

Blackwell, Roger, D. (1997) *Mind to Market*, Harper Business. One of many books by the leading authority on consumer behavior and author of the well-known Marketing textbook of the same name.

Branson, Richard, in *Forbes*, 3 July (2000). Whether you like him or not, whether it works or not, no marketing book is complete without some reference to this English entrepreneur and global gadabout. Find out more about him - he isn't always right - he's just always outrageous, and will make you think!

Brower, Charles, *Sales and Marketing*, "First Books for Business," McGraw-Hill, New York, (1996). A comic book treatment of the subject, but filled with pithy insights and useful information. Ideal for the beginner with a short attention span and a desire to get the fast and easy overview.

Christenson, Clayton and Tedlow, Richard S. (January–February (2000)) *Harvard Business Review*. A brilliant article related to the book *The Innovator's Dilemma*. Read the article first and, if that's not enough, get Christenson's book and read it to learn how upstarts upset entrenched industry leaders.

*Drucker, Peter F. (April (2000)) "Knowledge Work." *Executive Excellence*.

Drucker, Peter, F. (15 May (2000)) *Forbes*, pp. 88–89–. His irascible genius shows up all over the place.

Drucker, Peter F. (1999) *Management Challenges for the 21st Century*. Harper Business, New York. The leading management thinker of the twentieth century, and a prolific author of many books. He is not a marketing specialist, but so much of this insight goes to the heart of marketing that reading his books and other works is a valuable and enriching experience.

Fine, Charles H. (1998) *Clock Speed*. Perseus, Reading, MA. More of a supply chain book than a marketing one, but the principles of "speed" are worth knowing about.

*Gardial, Sarah and Woodruff, Robert (1996) *Know Your Customer*. Blackwell, Oxford. This is a deep and useful book about understanding what creates customer value, and how to determine what it is about the value that is compelling, and why. Written by professors, but rooted in strong real-world relationships with some leading companies. An excellent market-research-oriented reference.

Gilder, George (January (2000)) *Gilder Technology Report*. If you don't know what Telecosm and Microcosm mean, go to the archives of Forbes magazine's supplement ASAP and read Gilder's work circa (1997)-(2000).

Godin, Seth (1999) *Permission Marketing*. Simon & Schuster, New York. An irreverent, but refreshing new set of thoughts about marketing in the era of an empowered and widely dispersed customer base, written by one of the founding marketing gurus of Yahoo!

*Hamel, Gary and Prahalad, C.K. (1994) *Competing for the Future*. Harvard Business School Press, Boston, MA. This is a landmark work, and a must read for anyone interested in strategy - marketing or otherwise.

Hamel, Gary (April (2000)) "Conceptual Thinking," *Executive Excellence*.

Hamel, Gary (6 June 2000) *Wall Street Journal*. Attention revolutionaries - here is your leader! Check out his new book, *Leading the Revolution*, Harvard Business School Press, (2000),. . . but remember that failed revolutionaries usually get hanged - or at least fired - so proceed with caution.

Heil, Gary, Parker, Tom and Stevens, Deborah (1997) *One Size Fits One*. Wiley, New York. One of the early books recognizing the power of personalized marketing, and one which was early in the Internet era - but still appropriate.

Hisrich, Robert D. (1990) *Marketing*. Barron's Business Library. Dry as a dictionary, but a good place to find something about nearly everything. Not for recreational reading, but a decent reference.

Kelly, Kevin (1998) *New Rules for a New Economy*. Viking, New York. Strap on your digital thinking cap when you open a Kevin Kelly book. The editor of *Wired* magazine is a kick to read, and will stimulate new thoughts and ideas, whether you agree with him or not.

*Levitt, Theodore (1983) and (1986) *The Marketing Imagination*. The Free Press, New York. A must read for anyone serious about marketing. Some of the best marketing thought of the latter part of the twentieth century.

Mackay, Charles (1841) *Extraordinary Popular Delusions and the Madness of Crowds*. Not likely to find it - but accept it for its title alone.

McKenna, Regis (April (2000)) "Leadership in the Digital Age," *Executive Excellence*.

McKenna, Regis (1997) *Real Time*, Harvard Business School Press, Boston, MA. One of the early computer age gurus, he covers many key points about marketing in a real-time world.

Moore, Geoffrey, *Crossing the Chasm, Inside the Tornado*, and newer related works on strategy and execution involving marketing in the heart of the Silicon Valley technology era. If you are into this world, don't miss Moore's books.

Negroponte, Nicholas, *Being Digital*. While this book is "getting old" in an era when change is more rapid than ever, this book was so far ahead that it is still a fun, insightful read about how digital technology would change everything (and now has).

Palmatier, George E. and Shull, Joseph S. (1989) *The Marketing Edge*. Oliver Wight Limited Publications, Essex Junction, VT. Another book that is more supply-chain-oriented than most, but this one is from the granddaddy of the supply chain management organizations.

*Pine, B. Joseph and Gilmore, James (1999) *The Experience Economy*. Harvard Business School Press, Boston, MA. Pine and Gilmore coined the name and are now minting the ideas to go with it. These two books are fun, insightful and refreshingly full of ideas and conclusions in an age when everyone wants everything personalized, fun and easy.

Pine, B. Joseph (1993) *Mass Customization*. Harvard Business School Press, Boston, MA.

*Porter, Michael E. (1980) *Competitive Strategy*. The Free Press, New York. The seminal text on strategy in the 1980s. His newer writings in the *Harvard Business Review* expand and update his views, but this one laid the foundation.

*Ries, Al and Trout, Jack (1981) and (1986) *Positioning - The Battle for Your Mind*. McGraw-Hill, New York; and *The New Positioning* - anything that bears Ries' or Trout's name carries a lot of the wisdom of their great initial book, *Positioning - The Battle for Your Mind*, updated and restated. Even so, these are good, useful and enjoyable to read, and especially so for anyone in brands, advertising and promotion.

Ries, Al and Trout, Jack (April (2000)) *Rethinking the Future*, cited in *Executive Excellence*.

Ries, Al and Trout, Jack, *Marketing Warfare*. Not their best effort. Save your time unless you feel compelled to read everything on such topics - then read *The Art of War* by Sun Tzu.

Ries, Al and Ries Laura, *22 Immutable Laws of Branding*; and Ries, Laura, *The 11 Immutable Laws of Internet Branding* - both contain more of the same . . .

Schmitt, Bernd and Simonson, Alex (1997) *Marketing Aesthetics*. The Free Press, New York. Designers need to read these so they can quote them to their marketing brethren. Like all books that claim any one aspect of marketing reigns supreme, don't believe it all - but believe the parts they support with good factual information.

*Schultz, Don E., Tannenbaum, Stanley I. and Lauterborn, Robert F. (1993) *The New Marketing Paradigm*. NTC Business Books, Chicago, IL. An undiscovered treasure of good ideas from a group of Northwestern University professors. Easy to skim and find the treasures hidden in the text.

Tapscott, Don. A leading thinker about the implications of the digital era on everything, but especially the new youth of the digital generation and how they might evolve, to influence society and business for years to come - aptly summed up in his books and articles on *Digital Capital* and *Growing up Digital*.

Wallace, Thomas F. (1992) *Customer Driven Strategy*. Oliver Wight Publications, Essex Junction, VT. One of the supply chain guys crosses the road and gets in the minds of customers.

Ten Steps to Making it Work

In theory, there is little difference between theory and practice, but in practice, there is a great deal of difference. This chapter offers practical and specific steps that can be taken to enable a company to excel at marketing, and provides insight into some common errors to avoid.

The first step in marketing is to decide who you want to sell what, where, when and how much (and why you think you can). Either this is a new business that you must establish a need for, or it is a business where you must take share away from someone who already earned it - and won't give it up willingly.

1. A PLAN

The first of ten steps to making it all work is that the strategy of marketing has to match the strategy of the business. That means *you must have a plan* - a clear, concise, well-communicated plan - and then take action based on it. Too many times the plan is not well thought out, the target markets not well defined and the competition either underestimated or not fully researched.

Remedy all of those up front. Identify who has the business you want. Research the customers and the competition to determine what you will have to do to take the business you want. Define target markets prudently - neither too broadly nor too narrowly. Too broadly dilutes your resources. Too narrowly may yield an unsatisfactory result even if you are successful. And above all - communicate the plan to all those who must understand it to execute it - and listen closely to their feedback.

2. STRATEGY + EXECUTION

Strategy and execution must be closely integrated and well co-ordinated. *Match your strategy and execution*. If you have a well-conceived strategy, the steps of executing it should be evident. Think in terms of strategy defining "what" to do and the execution being "how" to do it. Assign clear responsibility for the various aspects of execution to specific people. Remember, if everyone is responsible, no *one* is really responsible!

Set specific measures of progress in the various steps of execution. These might include dates when product prototypes are approved, final tooling is finished, advertising strategy and budgets are determined, targeted customers are chosen, sales presentations are planned and rehearsed, early purchasing and production plans are set and communicated, and so forth.

Few things are more unfortunate than executing well against a weak strategy. One of the things that is clearly more unfortunate is to fail in execution against an excellent plan.

3. SERVE CUSTOMERS

Marketing is all about serving the customer, and to serve the customer, you must understand the customer's needs in all respects, *so get close to the customer*, and preferably get "inside their minds." There are many types of market research that can be done, but the first one is to listen to what the customer is telling you - or not telling you. Sometimes prospective customers do not want to give sales and marketing people the "bad news" about how they are really receiving the new product or program "pitch." If the customer avoids eye contact, gives vague or defensive answers and generally fails to show enthusiastic support - there may be a problem - like s/he doesn't like your product or doesn't want to abandon the current supplier, your competitor.

Market research with prospective consumers/end users is an important place to start. This will tell you what the ultimate purchaser considers to be "of value." There are many ways to do this: intercepts that compare similar products, focus groups, surveys, etc. One way which has proven quite effective is the "Customer Value Determination" process described in Woodruff & Gardial's book *Know Your Customer*.

If sales people have done a good job along the way getting to know the customers, and really listening to what they do and don't like about current or proposed products, then this task is much easier. But don't forget that all dealings between buyers and sellers are part of a negotiation process - and in negotiations, one of the parties may withhold or distort information to gain an advantage. That's why you must use multiple means to reach multiple levels of customers and consider all of their inputs.

4. COMMUNICATE

Communicate, communicate, communicate. I cannot emphasize this point enough. No one ever shares enough information and that is the one thing that unifies and empowers an organization. Communication is a two-way process. That means listen, make sure you understand what you hear correctly (and haven't translated it into what you wanted to hear!)

Learn to ask open-ended questions and communicate plans over and over, in both words and written form. Solicit input and feedback, and listen carefully. Involve everyone and, if in doubt, expand the circle of those involved the closer you get to the launch date of the product and/or marketing plan.

Communications must be done broadly, with customers, senior management, peer groups in sales, engineering, R & D, operations, and finance; in other words, with the entire organization that will be executing the plan, and serving the customer.

5. HOMEWORK

Always *do your homework*; do it fast and as well as you can in the time you have. There is more information out there than you think. Find it. Use it. In the rush to get to market ahead of a competitor, it is tempting to take shortcuts and not do the necessary homework! This was the undoing of many dot-com companies.

If you seek out all the places where information you might need is available, and do it well in advance, you'll know where to look when time is running out. One of the most often ignored pieces of homework is compiling a matrix of *"who sells whom,"* by product group and/or market segment. Everyone says they know this, but few can actually fill it out and make it balance to industry totals.

Without this homework you won't know with confidence where all of the available markets are, and who has them now. Neither will you consider who may be looking at your market share as a growth opportunity. Smart general managers insist on having this matrix completed and updated any time new information is discovered.

6. TALENT + PASSION

No talent, no passion means no success. *Everything depends on talented passionate people, working together*. One fact is certain - whoever has the best talent and a passionate organization with strong leadership will win in any competition. Mediocrity breeds mediocrity.

Remember the phrase, *"Good enough - isn't."* Even for industry leaders, perhaps especially for industry leaders, a talent or passion deficiency spells big trouble.

Not everyone in an organization can be a "star," but everyone must be competent, and there must be a greater than average number of high achievers if you hope to beat established competition. The other wonderful by-product of this kind of organization is that talent attracts more talent. The best in any field like to work with others who are equally talented. That makes recruiting a lot easier.

Passion is the one characteristic that can't be taught. It has to be felt, and once felt and shown/expressed, it can be contagious. Passion is what makes certain people rise above the rest and become great. The same goes for companies, and this is especially true when that passion infects the marketing organization.

7. RELATIONSHIPS

Marketing especially must *remember relationships*; first look "outside-in," but don't forget the inside relationships either. If talented people and passion are incredibly powerful marketing tools, then the extension of that thought is to infect others with the passion. No one can be good enough at everything these days. Business is too complex and fast moving. That means whoever chooses the best partners wins (all other things being equal), whether those partners are customers, suppliers or employees/associates.

Business success and marketing success are both all about building relationships based on trust and mutual respect. Customers are the first and most obvious relationships to remember and to build. These aren't the only ones. How about building relationships with non-customers that are good prospects? Then there are the underdeveloped relationships within companies. Marketing should be marketing their efforts inside the company almost as much as outside the company. These inside relationships are invaluable when it comes to serving the customers and sharing the passion.

8. SPEED + REACH

The Internet doesn't change *everything*, but what it does change is the ability and ways to *use the speed and reach of technology* in marketing. Just because the first wave of the Internet was riddled with early failures of dot-coms and e-companies does not mean that the technology era is over or unimportant.

Technology often cannot provide a competitive market advantage by its presence (alone). But its absence can create competitive disadvantages that can cripple the best of organizations. What technology makes possible is for marketers to know more, faster and about wider ranges of markets than ever before. Action on that knowledge is still required, but absent that knowledge, the action cannot even be considered.

No longer are marketing people and plans limited by distance and distribution of markets, as was once the case. In an MCI Network advertisement a few years ago, a prophetic line was used: "*There is no 'there' any more, there is only 'here' and we are all here ... on the network.*"

9. FAST BREAK

This section could be called *"Do it to them before they do it to you." Speed kills the competitors*. The principles like those used in the basketball fast break can stun, confuse and demoralize competitors. Marketing is the front ranks of competitive attack. If a company can plan and execute superbly and rapidly basing its moves on a clear understanding of the customer's needs, *and if it can beat the competitor to the punch - it wins BIG.*

Few strategic or tactical moves are more demoralizing than those based on speed. When Japanese auto makers shortened the new model development process to nearly half that of US makers, a large competitive advantage shifted to them. But rapid moves like basketball's fast breaks don't just happen. They are based on preparation, on doing homework, on choosing the right partners, and using the right technologies - and doing it all *faster* than the competitors.

At the rate of change in technology, product life cycles are getting shorter and shorter. Speed to market may be the only way to realize the full benefit of the returns on the marketing investment. Use it or lose it.

PP*2 ≠ FF (Protecting the Past and Perfecting the Present is not equal to Finding the Future.)

10. NEVER LOWER YOUR GUARD

Complacency or overconfidence kills more companies than competitors. Always assume you are under attack, because you are. The most vulnerable companies are the industry leaders, because they have the most to lose. Leaders are usually too invested in doing what they do better and better, that they don't look for the next new breakthrough. The first time they see is when they lose market share to it in big chunks. *Protecting the Past and Perfecting the Present is not a good path to Finding the Future*, yet that is exactly what most industry incumbents, especially the current leaders, are doing!

The best defense is a good offense, and the best offense is to take good care of customers. It is hard to attack when you are being attacked. That means a continuous attacking marketing strategy is superior to a defensive one. The ones to attack are competitors. The way to do that is to take superb care of the most important group of people in any marketer's professional life - customers. Remember Theodore Levitt's words, *"The purpose of a business is to create and keep a customer"* and I'll only add one word to that . . . *"happy!"*

SUMMARY

Here they are again . . . in condensed form for fast reference. Read them and heed them. Shortcuts are usually the longest path between two points and are filled with pitfalls.

1 The strategy of marketing has to match the strategy of the business. That means *you must have a plan* - a clear, concise, well-communicated plan and then take action based on it.
2 Strategy and execution must be closely integrated and well coordinated. *Match your strategy and execution.*
3 Marketing is all about serving the customer and, to serve the customer, you must understand the customer's needs in all respects, so *get close to the customer*, and preferably get "inside their minds."
4 *Communicate, communicate, communicate.* I cannot emphasize this point enough. No one ever shares enough information and that is the one thing that unifies and empowers an organization.

5 Always *do your homework*; do it fast and as well as you can in the time you have. There is more information out there than you think. Find it. Use it.
6 No talent, no passion means no success. *Everything depends on talented, passionate people working together*.
7 Marketing especially must *remember relationships*; first look outside in, but don't forget the inside relationships either.
8 The Internet doesn't change *everything*, but what it does change is the ability and ways to *use the speed and reach of technology*.
9 Do it to them before they do it to you. *Speed kills the competitors*.
10 *Never lower your guard*. Complacency or overconfidence kills more companies than competitors. Always assume you are under attack, because you always are.

Finally, for the last thought of *Marketing Express*, remember PP*2 ≠ FF! If you and your company are busy "protecting the past" or "perfecting the present," you won't have time or resources for "finding the future" - and everything that happens from here on will be - in the *future*! Where do you think your priorities and resources should be focused?

Frequently Asked Questions (FAQs)

Q1: What is marketing all about? How is it even definable?

A: See Chapter 1 – Introduction and Chapter 2 – Definition of Terms.

Q2: How is marketing different from sales? From product development?

A: See Chapter 2 – Definition of Terms.

Q3: What do all of those acronyms mean that the advertising and marketing people are always throwing around?

A: See Chapter 8 – Key Concepts and Thinkers.

Q4: The Internet explosion created all of these new marketing concepts. Are any of them still valid?

A: See Chapter 4 – The E-Dimension.

Q5: What all goes into a marketing plan?

A: See Chapter 2 – Definition of Terms.

Q6: Where can I learn something about brands and branding?

A: See Chapter 6 - The State of the Art.

Q7: Is marketing pretty much the same all over the world?

A: See Chapter 5 - The Global Dimension.

Q8: Are there a few examples of companies that have done marketing well?

A: See Chapter 6 - The State of the Art and Chapter 7 - In Practice.

Q9: Are there a few simple rules I can learn that will help me be successful in marketing?

A: See Chapter 10 - Ten Steps to Making it Work.

Q10: I'm pressed for time - what must I read to get the most important message from this book in the least amount of time?

A: See Chapter 1 - Introduction and Chapter 10 - Ten Steps to Making it Happen.

Index